summer

recipe collection

by **Sainsbury's**

100 delicious recipes for everyday inspiration

Welcome...

...to the summer recipe collection by Sainsbury's. We've put together a stunning selection of irresistible recipes, to give you everyday inspiration all summer long, whatever the occasion.

Each delicious recipe has been tried, tested and tasted by Sainsbury's, so you can be sure of great results, whatever your level of cooking expertise. All the dishes are made from readily available ingredients, with easy-to-follow, step-by-step instructions. The recipes are divided into clear sections, from soups and snacks through to mains and desserts, so it's easy to find just what you need to feed your family. Summer should be all about fun, so there's also a great selection of tasty barbecue recipes and a handy picnic section to help you get the most from the longer days.

Prep times, cooking times and nutritional information are provided for each recipe, and we also flag up recipes containing one or more of your 5 a day, to help you make healthier choices. And, as the last thing you probably want to do when the sun's shining is spend hours in the kitchen, many of these recipes can be on the table in 45 minutes or less.

We hope you find plenty of inspiration to create fabulous meals, and that this cookbook becomes an indispensable addition to your kitchen. Have a great summer!

We've added these icons to make everything as clear as possible

(45 mins) Recipes that can be on the table in 45 minutes or less

(V) Suitable for vegetarians

(2 of 5 A-DAY) Recipes containing 1 or more of your 5 a day, to help you plan for healthy eating

contents

■ Soups & snacks   6

■ Salads   24

■ Summer dinners   52

■ Fish & seafood   82

■ Barbecues   116

■ Picnics   142

■ Desserts   164

soups
& snacks

Summer vegetable soup with croutons	8
Gazpacho	10
Sweetcorn chowder with prawns	12
Avocado, salami & cherry tomato bruschetta	14
Gruyère & ham quesadillas	16
Minty broad bean pâté	18
Guacamole	18
Cheesy nachos	20
Spiced pitta crisps & houmous	20
Roasted thyme tomatoes with griddled crusty bread	22
Smoked mackerel pâté with cucumber salad	22

Serves 6
Prep time: 10 minutes
Cook time: 10 minutes

Summer vegetable soup with croutons

A swirl of pesto adds extra flavour to the spring vegetables in this soup, and the ciabatta croutons make tasty accompaniments

---

2 teaspoons olive oil

1 red onion, peeled and chopped

1½ litres vegetable stock (for meat eaters you could use chicken stock)

100g frozen peas

100g green beans, chopped

1 medium courgette, cut into small cubes

200g cherry tomatoes, halved

6 slices Taste the Difference ciabatta

3 tablespoons green pesto sauce

---

1 Preheat the grill to medium-high.

2 Heat 1 teaspoon olive oil in a large saucepan over a medium heat. Add the onion and cook gently until translucent (not golden).

3 Pour in the stock and bring to a simmer. Add the peas, beans, courgette and tomatoes, and simmer for about 5 minutes, until just tender. Meanwhile, brush the ciabatta with the remaining 1 teaspoon oil, then toast under the grill.

4 Pour the soup into 6 bowls. Stir ½ tablespoon pesto into each and serve with a ciabatta crouton on the side.

Per serving: 206 cals, 8.3g fat, 1.6g sat fat, 4.3g total sugars, trace salt

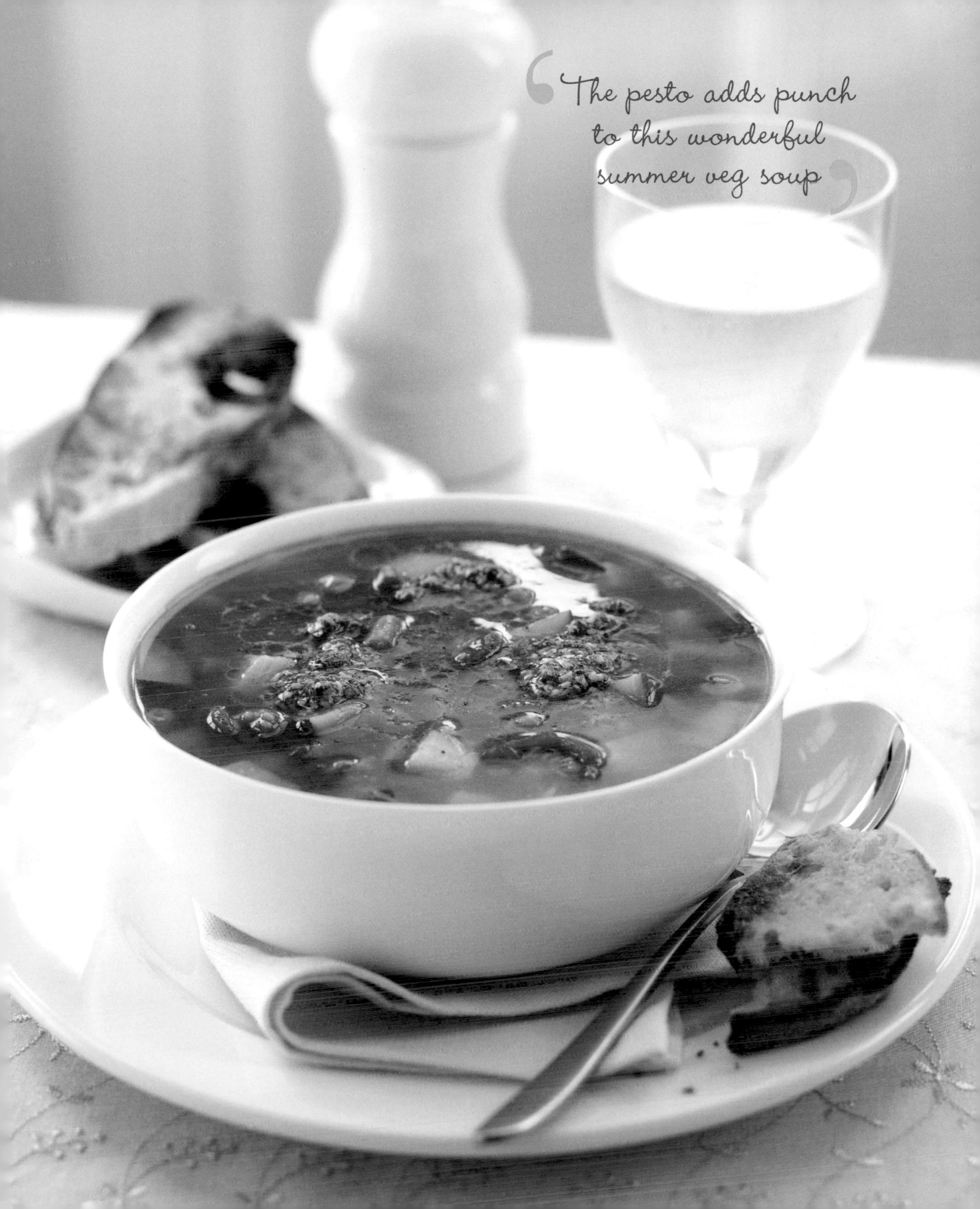
'The pesto adds punch to this wonderful summer veg soup'

Serves 4
Prep time: 15 minutes, plus chilling time

Gazpacho

This quick and easy chilled soup is the perfect cooling starter on a hot day. It also tastes lovely heated up when the weather turns chilly

1 x 700g jar Sainsbury's SO organic passata
2 red peppers, deseeded and chopped
1 red chilli, deseeded and chopped
2 cloves garlic, peeled and crushed
2 teaspoons mild chilli powder
2 tablespoons red wine vinegar

juice of 1 lime
50g cucumber, finely chopped
¼ x red onion, peeled and finely chopped
1 tablespoon fresh coriander, chopped
4 tablespoons half-fat crème fraîche

1 Whizz the passata, peppers, fresh chilli and garlic in a food processor or blender until smooth. Pour into a jug and chill in the fridge for at least 30 minutes.

2 Just before serving, mix through the chilli powder, red wine vinegar and lime juice. Season to taste with salt and freshly ground black pepper. In a bowl, mix together the cucumber, onion, coriander and crème fraîche, then season with salt and freshly ground black pepper.

3 Pour the soup into 4 bowls, topping each one with a spoonful of the crème fraîche mixture. You could add an ice cube or two to each bowl to keep the soup perfectly chilled.

Per serving: 125 cals, 3.5g fat, 2g sat fat, 14.7g total sugars, 1.3g salt

Try this soup warm...
Heat the blended passata, pepper, chilli and garlic in a pan, then add the chilli powder, red wine vinegar and lime juice. Season. Top with the crème fraîche mixture and serve

'This Spanish-style, chilled soup is perfect for a summer day'

Serves 4
Prep time: 20 minutes
Cook time: 35 minutes

Sweetcorn chowder with prawns

This creamy prawn and sweetcorn soup is substantial enough for a main course

2 teaspoons olive oil
1 teaspoon butter
1 onion, peeled and finely chopped
1 clove garlic, peeled and sliced
1 teaspoon Dijon mustard
½ teaspoon paprika
2 tablespoons plain flour
500ml vegetable stock, cooled

2 potatoes, peeled and cubed
4 sweetcorn cobs, kernels only
300ml semi-skimmed milk
100ml single cream
1 x 180g pack Sainsbury's raw peeled king prawns
½ x 28g pack Sainsbury's fresh flat-leaf parsley, chopped

1 Heat the oil and butter in a large saucepan. Add the onion, garlic, mustard and paprika and fry for about 5 minutes, until softened.

2 Sprinkle in the flour and stir until absorbed. Remove from the heat and add the stock in batches, stirring each time until smooth. Return to the heat and add the potatoes.

3 Bring to the boil then reduce the heat and simmer, stirring occasionally, for 10-15 minutes, until the potatoes are cooked. Add the corn and simmer for a further 5 minutes.

4 Pour in the milk and cream, then add the prawns. Heat for about 5 minutes, until the prawns are pink and cooked - do not boil.

5 Stir through the chopped parsley. Season to taste with salt and freshly ground black pepper, then pour into bowls to serve.

Per serving: 352 cals, 14.7g fat, 5.3g sat fat, 9.2g total sugars, 1g salt

“This creamy, colourful soup is wonderfully rich and satisfying”

soups & snacks

Serves 4
(2 slices each)
Prep time: 10 minutes
Cook time: 5 minutes

Avocado, salami & cherry tomato bruschetta

These toasted ciabatta slices, topped with a medley of Mediterranean flavours, are ideal for a starter or lunch or for sharing at summer parties

8 cherry tomatoes, quartered
1 teaspoon red or white wine vinegar
1 large avocado
squeeze of lemon juice
8 slices Taste the Difference ciabatta, sliced on the diagonal

1 clove garlic, peeled but left whole
1 tablespoon extra virgin olive oil
4 slices Sainsbury's Italian Milano salami, each sliced into 3 strips
shavings of parmesan
handful of Sainsbury's wild rocket leaves

1 Heat a griddle pan or preheat your grill to medium-high. In a bowl, mix together the tomatoes and vinegar. Peel and stone the avocado, then mash with the lemon juice in a bowl.

2 Toast the ciabatta slices on the griddle pan or under the grill. Remove, then rub one side of each with the garlic clove and drizzle with olive oil.

3 Spread the ciabatta slices with the mashed avocado. Top with the tomatoes, slivers of salami, parmesan shavings and rocket leaves, then serve.

Per serving: 327 cals, 17.9g fat, 3.6g sat fat, 2.9g total sugars, 0.2g salt

Try some different toppings...
These toppings also work well on bruschetta:
• pesto, mozzarella and prosciutto
• broad bean, pea and feta, mashed into a pâté

14

Serves 8
Prep time: 10 minutes
Cook time: 8 minutes

Gruyère & ham quesadillas

Full of tasty vegetables, ham and melting cheese, these Mexican-inspired toasties are great as a starter or snack

8 soft flour tortillas
50g young leaf spinach
150g Gruyère cheese or mature Cheddar, grated
100g Taste the Difference SunBlush® tomatoes, chopped

3 large spring onions, trimmed and sliced
1 avocado, peeled, stoned and chopped
150g sliced ham, chopped
1 tablespoon sunflower oil
sliced jalapeno peppers, to serve
salsa, to serve

1 Place 4 of the tortillas on a clean surface. Divide the spinach, cheese, tomatoes, spring onions, avocado and ham between them. Season with salt and freshly ground black pepper and top each with another tortilla to make the quesadillas.

2 Heat a large frying pan over a medium heat and oil very lightly with a little of the sunflower oil. Add a quesadilla and cook for 1 minute on each side, or until golden and crisp. Wrap in foil and keep warm while you continue cooking the remaining quesadillas, adding more oil to the pan if necessary.

3 Cut each quesadilla into 8 wedges and serve with jalapeno peppers and a spoonful of salsa.

Per serving: 352 cals, 18.8g fat, 7.5g sat fat, 2.7g total sugars, 1.5g salt

Did you know...?
All of Sainsbury's fresh ham is 100% British (except Parma ham)

Minty broad bean pâté

Serves 4
Prep time: 10 minutes,
plus peeling (optional)
Cook time: 4 minutes

This simple pâté is packed with summery flavour. It's delicious on toasted baguette with rocket leaves and a drizzle of olive oil

350g broad beans (podded weight)
1 x 250g pot Sainsbury's ricotta cheese
1 x 28g pack Sainsbury's fresh mint,
leaves only

1 tablespoon extra virgin olive oil
zest and juice of 1 small lemon
12 slices ciabatta, toasted, to serve
rocket leaves, to serve

1 Cook the broad beans in boiling salted water for 3–4 minutes, until tender. Drain and cool under cold running water. When cool, peel off the skins, if you wish.

2 Place the beans, ricotta, mint, oil, lemon zest and juice in a food processor and blend to a rough purée. Season well with salt and freshly ground black pepper. Great served on toasted ciabatta, garnished with rocket leaves.

Per serving: 177 cals, 9.9g fat, 4.7g sat fat, 3.4g total sugars, 0.2g salt

Guacamole

Mash the flesh of 2 ripe avocados in a bowl with the juice of 1 lime. Add 1 peeled, crushed clove garlic, 1/2 teaspoon cumin and a drop of Tabasco® (optional) and mix well. Season with salt and freshly ground black pepper, then add 1/2 x deseeded, finely chopped red chilli, 1/2 x small red onion, peeled and finely chopped, and 1/2 x 250g pack Sainsbury's vine-ripened tomatoes, chopped. Great served with tortilla wraps cut into stars or triangles and baked until golden.

SERVES 6 Prep time: 20 minutes

Per serving: 106 cals, 9.6g fat, 2g sat fat, 1.6g total sugars, trace salt

'The fresh flavours of
broad beans and mint
make a fantastic pâté'

Serves 4
Prep time: 10 minutes
Cook time: 8 minutes

Cheesy nachos

Summer food is all about easy ideas that are made for sharing, and these nachos are just the thing for everyone to dip into

1 x 230g pot Sainsbury's chunky salsa dip
1 x 200g bag Sainsbury's cool tortilla chips
4 spring onions, chopped

1 x 125g pack Sainsbury's basics mozzarella pearls
2 tablespoons fresh flat-leaf parsley, chopped

1 Preheat the oven to 200°C, fan 180°C, gas 6. Spoon some of the salsa dip into a small bowl for dipping.

2 Place half the tortilla chips in an ovenproof dish and top with half the remaining salsa dip and half the spring onions and mozzarella pearls.

3 Repeat with a second layer of tortilla chips, salsa dip, spring onions and mozzarella pearls. Bake for 5-8 minutes, until the cheese melts.

4 Sprinkle with the parsley and serve with the bowl of salsa for dipping.

Per serving: 357 cals, 19.1g fat, 9.4g sat fat, 4.6g total sugars, 1.1g salt

Spiced pitta crisps & houmous

Preheat the oven to 200°C, fan 180°C, gas 6. In a bowl, mix 3 tablespoons olive oil with ½ teaspoon each ground cumin, ground coriander and paprika, and season. Briefly toast 3 white pittas until hot and puffed up but not golden. Carefully split open the pittas and brush the spiced oil onto the cut sides. Cut into fingers and bake on a baking tray for 6-7 minutes, until golden and crisp. Serve on a platter with 1 x 200g pot Sainsbury's Moroccan style houmous.

SERVES 4 Prep time: 10 minutes Cook time: 7 minutes

Per serving: 301 cals, 17.7g fat, 4.6g sat fat, 2.2g total sugars, 0.8g salt

Serves 4
Prep time: 15 minutes
Cook time: 1 hour,
5 minutes

Roasted thyme tomatoes

with griddled crusty bread

These tasty tomatoes are also great on pizzas or with pasta or roast chicken

2 x 250g packs Sainsbury's vine-ripened tomatoes, halved
2 cloves garlic, peeled and chopped

1 tablespoon fresh thyme leaves
3 tablespoons olive oil
12 slices crusty white bread, to serve

1 Preheat the oven to 150°C, fan 130°C, gas 2.

2 Arrange the tomatoes on a baking tray and scatter over the garlic and thyme. Drizzle over 1 tablespoon oil and roast in the oven for 1 hour.

3 Drizzle the bread with the remaining 2 tablespoons oil and season with salt and freshly ground black pepper. Heat a griddle pan until hot and cook the bread for 2-3 minutes on each side, until golden. Top with the tomatoes and serve at once.

Per serving: 373 cals, 10.8g fat, 1.3g sat fat, 6.9g total sugars, 1.4g salt

Smoked mackerel pâté
with cucumber salad

Mix 1 peeled, thinly sliced cucumber with 2 teaspoons sea salt. Refrigerate for 1 hour. Flake 4 skinned smoked mackerel fillets into a bowl. Fold in 4 tablespoons half-fat crème fraîche, 2-3 tablespoons horseradish sauce, the zest of 1 lemon and black pepper. Drain the cucumber and stir in 1 x 20g pack dill, chopped, the juice of 1 lemon and 2 teaspoons sugar. Serve with the pâté, lemon wedges and toasted ciabatta.

SERVES 8 Prep time: 20 minutes, plus chilling time

Per serving: 398 cals, 26.7g fat, 6g sat fat, 3.7g total sugars, 2.5g salt

salads

Oriental honey roast chicken salad	26
Greek salad	28
Salmon & cucumber salad	28
Grilled sweetcorn, spinach & pancetta salad	30
Asparagus & mozzarella salad	32
Smoked salmon & asparagus niçoise	34
Spicy three-bean salad with halloumi	36
Artichoke & broad bean salad	38
Fruity & nutty couscous salad	40
Prawn, mango & noodle salad	42
Tomato, red onion & mint salad	44
Stacked BLT salad	44
Bacon, asparagus & poached egg salad	46
Rocket & chilli squid salad	48
Lamb & bulgar wheat salad	50

Oriental honey roast chicken salad

Serves 4
Prep time: 30 minutes, plus marinating time
Cook time: 20 minutes

1 of 5 A-DAY

This warm, vibrant salad is full of tempting oriental flavours

3 tablespoons runny honey

2 tablespoons soy sauce

3cm piece fresh ginger, peeled and finely grated

1 clove garlic, peeled and finely grated

1 red chilli, deseeded and finely chopped

4 Taste the Difference free-range chicken breasts, skin on

1 x 300g pack Sainsbury's rice noodles

1 tablespoon olive oil

juice of $\frac{1}{2}$ x lemon

70g mixed salad leaves

1 bunch spring onions, sliced

1 x 270g pack Taste the Difference vittoria tomatoes on the vine, halved

1 In a large bowl, mix together the honey, soy sauce, ginger, garlic and half the red chilli, to make the glaze. Add the chicken. Place in the fridge to marinate for about 1 hour.

2 Meanwhile, preheat the oven to 200ºC, fan 180ºC, gas 6. Line a baking tray or shallow roasting tin with kitchen foil. Reserving the marinade, place the chicken skin-side up on the foil – some of the glaze should be sticking to the meat. Cook in the oven for 10 minutes, then remove and spoon the remaining marinade over the skin. Cook for a further 10 minutes, until the skin is crispy.

3 Meanwhile, soak the rice noodles in boiling water, following pack instructions. Drain, then toss with the olive oil, remaining chilli and lemon juice.

4 Slice the cooked chicken breasts diagonally. Toss together the salad leaves, spring onions, tomatoes and noodles. Divide between 4 plates and arrange the sliced chicken breasts on top of the salad.

Per serving: 411 cals, 11.9g fat, 3.6g sat fat, 13.4g total sugars, 1.7g salt

'Honey, ginger and chilli create a flavoursome glaze for the chicken'

Greek salad

Transport yourself to a sun-drenched Greek island with this tasty side salad

½ x 200g pack Sainsbury's Greek feta
5 vine tomatoes, each cut into wedges
100g olives (try Sainsbury's dry black olives
and Kalamata olives)
½ x red onion, peeled and sliced

FOR THE DRESSING
2 tablespoons oil
1½ tablespoons lemon juice
pinch salt
large pinch cayenne
pinch sugar

1   In a large bowl, mix together the feta, tomatoes, olives and slices of red onion.

2   Combine all the dressing ingredients in a small bowl, then drizzle over the salad just before serving.

Per serving: 224 cals, 19.2g fat, 5.7g sat fat, 3.9g total sugars, 3.8g salt

Tip
For an even easier salad, use Sainsbury's be good to yourself French dressing instead of making your own

Salmon & cucumber salad

Boil 500g new potatoes, then drain and cool. Rub 300g skinless & boneless salmon fillets with 1 tablespoon oil and season with salt and freshly ground black pepper. Place on a microwaveable plate, cover with clingfilm and cook on high for 3½ minutes. When cool, break into chunks. Toss with the potatoes, 1 thinly sliced cucumber, 100ml half-fat crème fraîche, 15g chopped fresh dill and the juice of 1 lemon.

SERVES 4 Prep time: 10 minutes Cook time: 15 minutes

Per serving: 321 cals, 16.4g fat, 6.7g sat fat, 3.9g total sugars, 0.2g salt

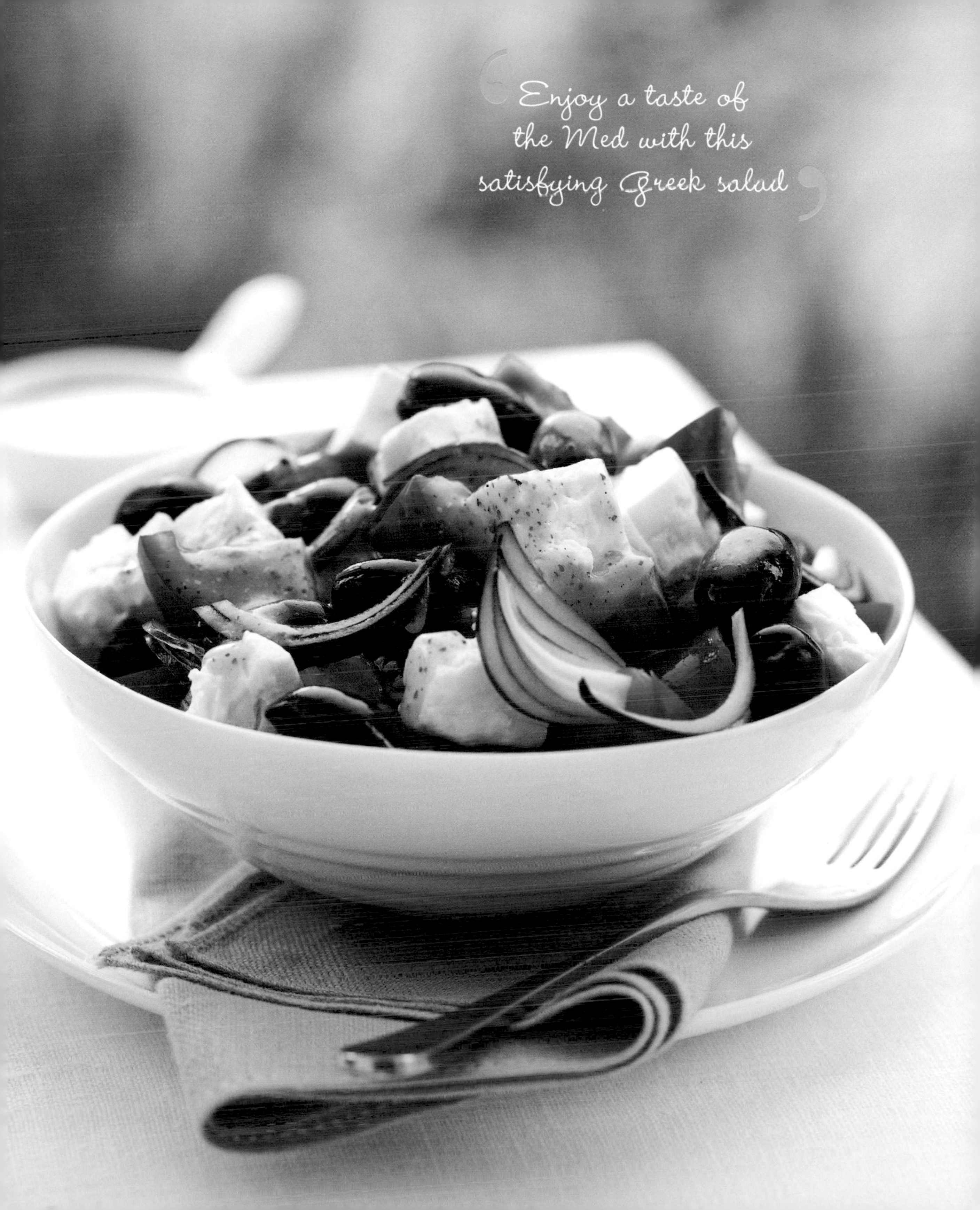
'Enjoy a taste of
the Med with this
satisfying Greek salad'

Serves 4
Prep time: 10 minutes
Cook time: 5 minutes

Grilled sweetcorn, spinach & pancetta salad

Tender and tasty, the season's sweetcorn is a delicious addition to spinach leaves and crispy pancetta in this colourful salad

2 sweetcorn cobs, each cut into 4
4 tablespoons olive oil
1 x 105g pack Sainsbury's smoked pancetta
150g young leaf spinach

½ x red onion, peeled and sliced
1 tablespoon white wine vinegar
2 teaspoons wholegrain mustard

1 Preheat the grill.

2 Meanwhile, heat a griddle pan. Toss the sweetcorn pieces with 1 tablespoon olive oil, then grill on the hot griddle pan until charred. (Alternatively, you could grill them on a barbecue.) Season with salt and freshly ground black pepper.

3 Heat the pancetta under the grill until crispy. Remove and tear into pieces. Place in a large bowl with the sweetcorn, spinach and red onion slices, and toss together.

4 In a small bowl, combine the remaining 3 tablespoons olive oil with the white wine vinegar and mustard. Serve the salad on a platter with the dressing drizzled over.

Per serving: 271 cals, 20.2g fat, 3.9g sat fat, 2.3g total sugars, 1.3g salt

Time-saving tip
Instead of making your own dressing for this salad, try using Sainsbury's be good to yourself honey & mustard dressing

This help-yourself salad is ideal for summer parties and barbecues

Serves 6
Prep time: 10 minutes
Cook time: 5 minutes

Asparagus & mozzarella salad

Dried apricots add a touch of sweetness to the fresh flavours of asparagus and watercress in this couscous salad

125g couscous
350g asparagus, washed and trimmed
1 x 125g pack Sainsbury's SO organic mozzarella, torn into bite-sized pieces
12 dried, ready to eat apricots, sliced

60ml extra virgin olive oil
juice of 1 lemon
4 sprigs fresh thyme, leaves picked and chopped
1 x 75g pack Sainsbury's watercress

1 Tip the couscous into a bowl. Pour in 150ml boiling water, cover with clingfilm and leave to stand for 5-10 minutes.

2 Meanwhile, blanch the asparagus in boiling salted water for 3-4 minutes, until tender, then drain and refresh under cold running water. Cut into 3cm pieces and place in a large bowl.

3 Add the mozzarella and apricots to the asparagus. Fluff the couscous with a fork and add to the mixture. Season with salt and freshly ground black pepper.

4 Whisk together the oil, lemon juice and thyme in a small jug, then toss with the couscous. Serve on a bed of watercress.

Per serving: 257 cals, 15.2g fat, 5.1g sat fat, 4.4g total sugars, 0.1g salt

“This salad makes the most of fresh seasonal flavours”

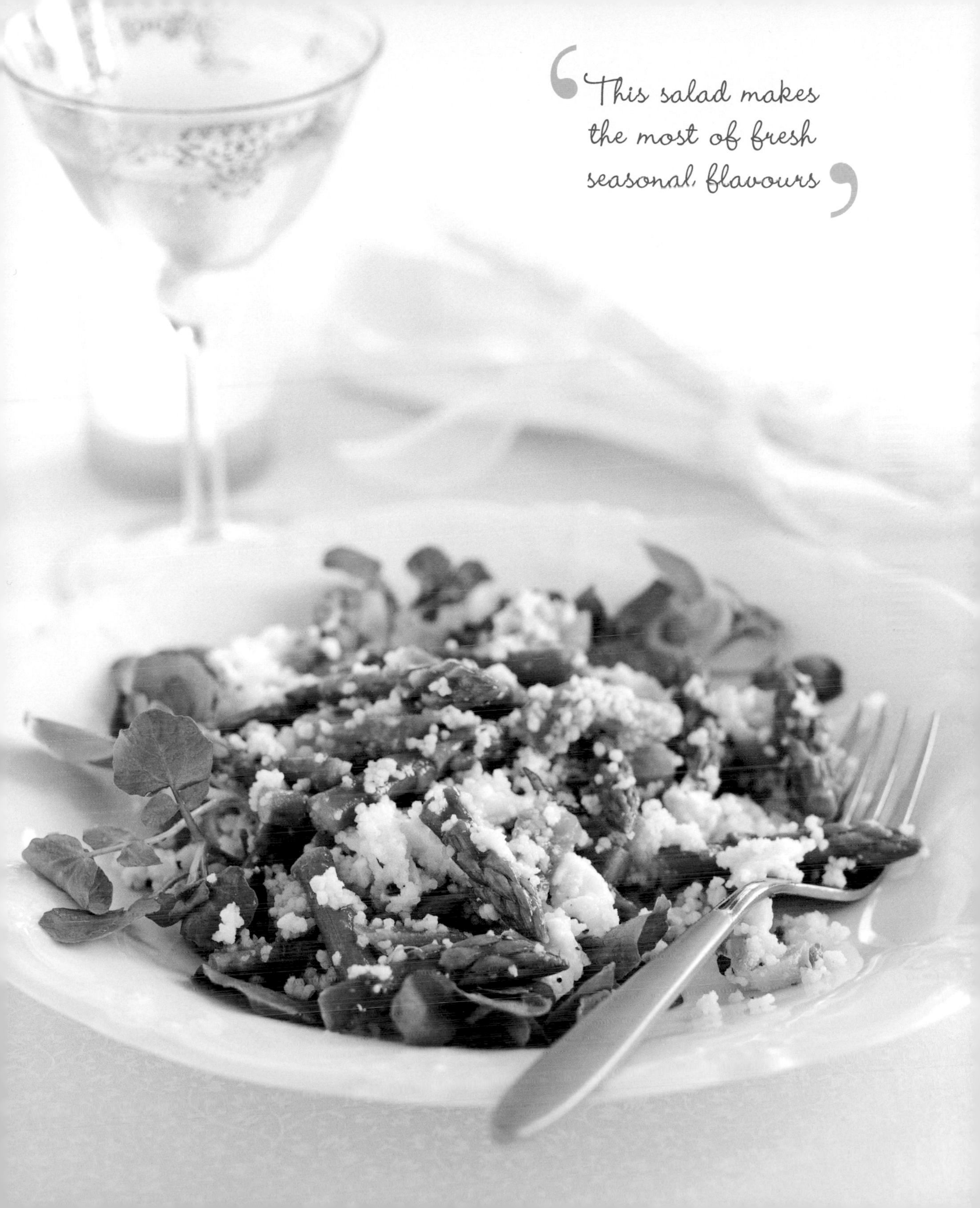

Serves 6
Prep time: 20 minutes
Cook time: 20 minutes

Smoked salmon & asparagus niçoise

Smoked salmon and asparagus add a twist to a classic niçoise salad

1 x 1kg pack Taste the Difference baby Jersey Royals, or new potatoes
250g asparagus, halved, woody ends removed
200g green beans, topped and tailed
100g pitted black and/or Kalamata olives
½ x red onion, peeled and finely sliced
4 hard-boiled free-range eggs, quartered

200g Taste the Difference smoked salmon, sliced into ribbons

FOR THE DRESSING
2 heaped tablespoons fresh dill, finely chopped
2 tablespoons extra virgin olive oil
1 tablespoon white wine vinegar
½ teaspoon caster sugar

1 Place the potatoes in a large pan of cold water and bring to the boil. Simmer for 15-20 minutes, until tender, then drain. Allow the potatoes to cool, then cut in half.

2 Meanwhile, blanch the asparagus and beans for 3 minutes in a pan of boiling water. Drain and place in a bowl of cold water for 10 minutes to set the colour, then drain.

3 In a bowl, mix together the ingredients for the dressing. Place the potatoes in a large bowl and toss with the asparagus, beans, olives, onion and dressing. Serve topped with the egg and salmon, and season with salt and freshly ground black pepper.

Per serving: 331 cals, 16.2g fat, 3.3g sat fat, 5.5g total sugars, 1.8g salt

Fair on fish
All Sainsbury's fresh and smoked salmon is 100% Scottish and reared on Freedom Food farms that meet RSPCA standards for welfare

"The fresh dill dressing
is the perfect partner
for smoked salmon"

Serves 4
Prep time: 10 minutes
Cook time: 20 minutes

Spicy three-bean salad with halloumi

Halloumi cheese is delicious grilled and works well with the three different types of beans in this protein-packed salad

1 x 250g pack Taste the Difference pomodorino tomatoes
2 shallots, peeled and chopped
2 tablespoons olive oil
300g green beans, trimmed and cut in half
1 x 410g tin Sainsbury's red kidney beans, drained and rinsed

1 x 410g tin Sainsbury's butter beans, drained and rinsed
1 red chilli, deseeded and finely chopped
juice of 1 lemon
1 tablespoon fresh thyme leaves
1 x 250g pack Sainsbury's Cypriot halloumi cheese, sliced
50g baby spinach

1 Preheat the oven to 180°C, fan 160°C, gas 4. Place the tomatoes and shallots in a roasting tray and drizzle with a little of the olive oil. Season to taste with salt and freshly ground black pepper and roast in the oven for 20 minutes.

2 Meanwhile, bring a pan of salted water to the boil and drop in the green beans. Cook for 4 minutes, then drain and refresh in cold water. Place in a large bowl, add the kidney beans and butter beans and toss together. Stir in the chilli, lemon juice, thyme leaves and remaining olive oil, then set aside to marinate.

3 Meanwhile, heat a grill or non-stick griddle pan to a medium heat and cook the halloumi for 2 minutes on each side, until golden and melting slightly.

4 Toss the roast tomatoes, roast shallots and spinach with the bean mixture and divide between 4 plates. Top each salad with slices of halloumi cheese. Great with pitta bread.

Per serving: 419 cals, 23.4g fat, 10.6g sat fat, 6.8g total sugars, 1.9g salt

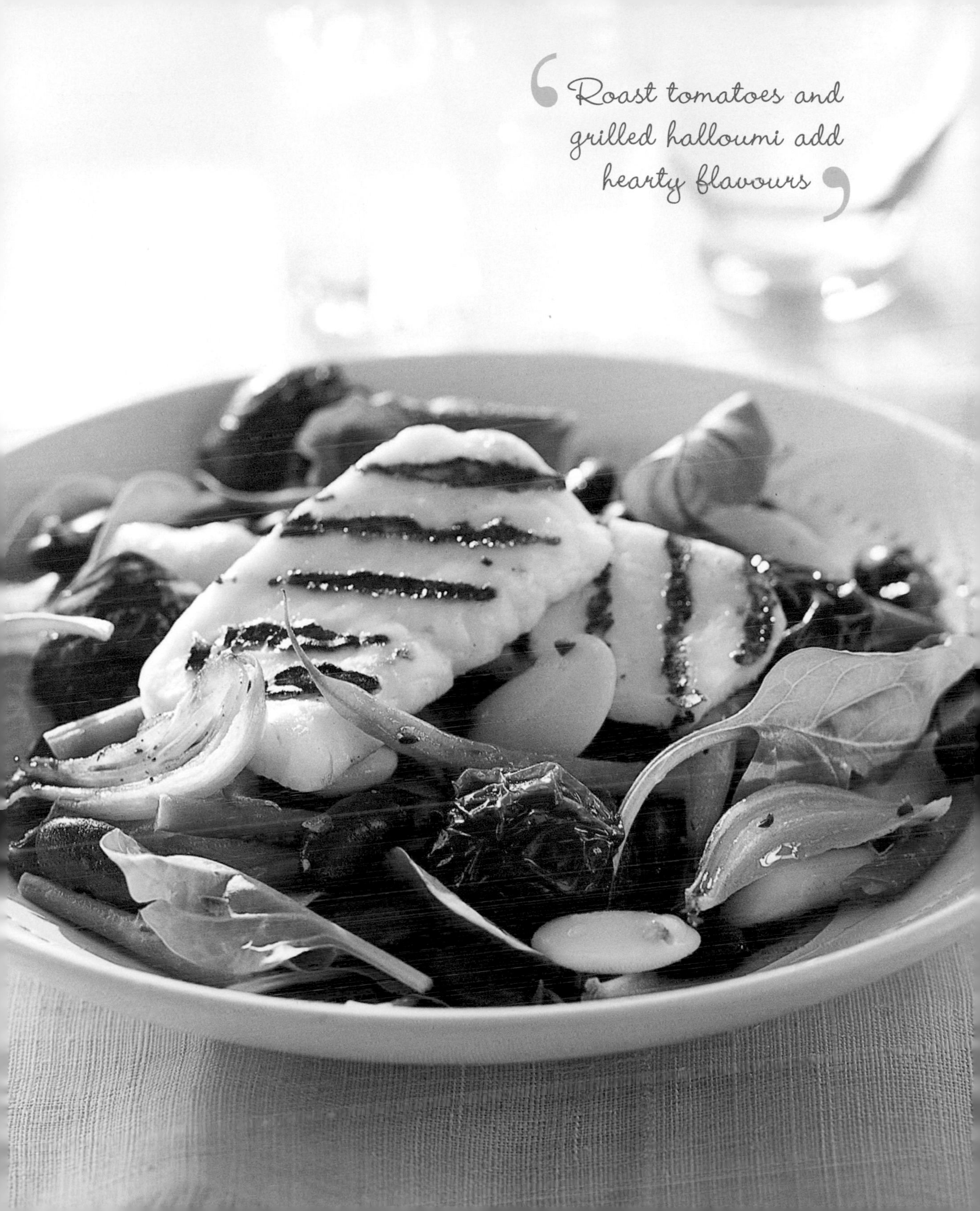
Roast tomatoes and grilled halloumi add hearty flavours

Artichoke & broad bean salad

Antipasti artichokes, broad beans and rosemary, with a dressing of olive oil and lemon juice, create a delicious Italian-inspired salad

2 x 280g jars Taste the Difference chargrilled artichokes in olive oil
300g broad beans, cooked and peeled

2 sprigs rosemary, leaves picked and chopped
juice of 1 lemon
parmesan shavings, to serve

1 Drain the artichokes and reserve the oil. Place the artichokes, broad beans and rosemary in a large bowl, and toss well together.

2 In a small jug, whisk the lemon juice with the olive oil reserved from the artichokes, and season with salt and freshly ground black pepper. Pour the dressing over the artichokes and beans. Scatter over the parmesan shavings to serve.

Per serving: 441 cals, 41.2g fat, 5.8g sat fat, 2.5g total sugars, 1.7g salt

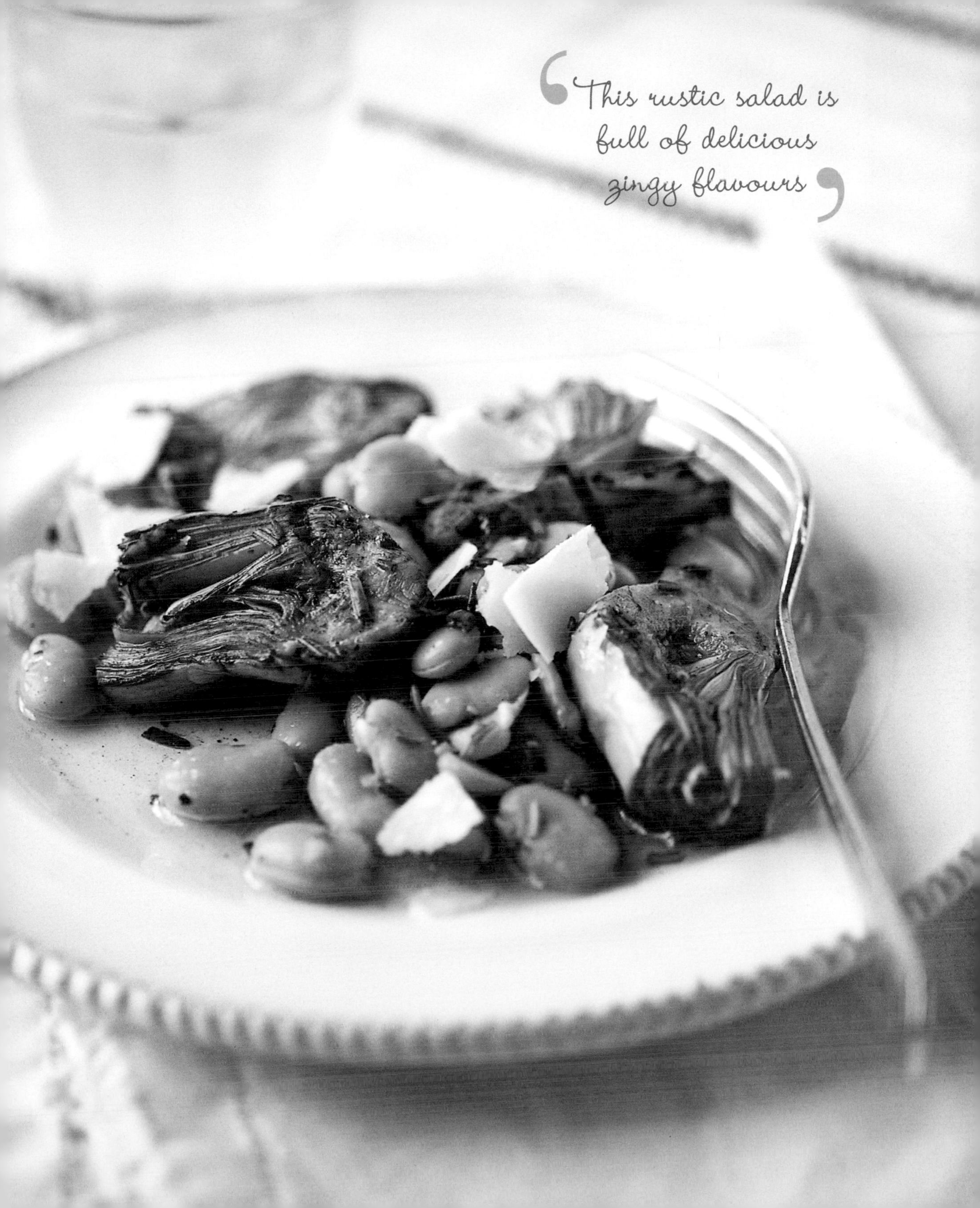

'This rustic salad is
full of delicious
zingy flavours'

Fruity & nutty couscous salad

This side salad is full of vitality and couldn't be easier to make – simply prepare the couscous and stir in all the ingredients

---

½ x 500g pack Sainsbury's couscous
100g whole pistachio nuts, shelled
100g dried, ready to eat apricots, halved
1 x 410g tin Sainsbury's chick peas, drained and rinsed
1 bunch spring onions, finely sliced

4 tablespoons raisins
1 x 28g pack Sainsbury's fresh coriander, chopped
juice of 1 lemon
1 tablespoon extra virgin olive oil

---

1 Place the couscous in a large bowl. Pour in 300ml boiling water, cover with clingfilm and leave to stand for 5-10 minutes.

2 When the couscous is cool, add the remaining ingredients. Season with salt and freshly ground black pepper and toss together.

Per serving: 305 cals, 9.2g fat, 1.2g sat fat, 15.7g total sugars, trace salt

Serves 1
Prep time: 10 minutes
Cook time: 5 minutes

Prawn, mango & noodle salad

A dressing of sweet chilli sauce, soy sauce and lime juice adds a kick to the fresh flavours in this Thai-inspired, single-serve salad

50g mange tout
100g tenderstem broccoli
85g rice noodles
½ x 225g pack Taste the Difference cooked jumbo king prawns
3 spring onions, sliced

½ x medium ripe mango, peeled and diced
½ x 28g pack Sainsbury's fresh mint, leaves picked and chopped
1½ tablespoons sweet chilli sauce
1 teaspoon reduced-salt soy sauce
juice of ½ x lime

1 Blanch the mange tout and broccoli in boiling water for 3-4 minutes. Drain and cool under cold running water.

2 Meanwhile, soak the noodles in boiling water for 2 minutes, then drain and cool under cold running water.

3 In a large bowl, toss together the noodles, cooked vegetables, prawns, spring onions, mango and mint.

4 To make the dressing, whisk together the sweet chilli sauce, soy sauce and lime juice in a bowl. Pour the dressing over the salad, toss to combine and serve immediately.

Per serving: 358 cals, 4.2g fat, 0.5g sat fat, 26.9g total sugars, 2.5g salt

For a change...
Shredded chicken pieces, slices of rare beef or cubes of tofu work equally as well as prawns with the delicate Thai flavours of this dish

Vibrant veg, prawns and noodles create an appetising salad

Tomato, red onion & mint salad

Flavoursome and juicy, British tomatoes are one of the highlights of summer, and they take centre stage in this fabulous side salad

1 x 250g pack Taste the Difference vine tomatoes, roughly chopped
1 x 28g pack Sainsbury's fresh mint, leaves picked and finely chopped

½ x red onion, peeled and sliced
2 tablespoons extra virgin olive oil
1 tablespoon white wine vinegar

1 In a large bowl, toss the tomatoes with the mint and red onion.

2 In a small bowl, mix together the olive oil and white wine vinegar. Season with salt and freshly ground black pepper, then drizzle over the salad.

3 Arrange on a serving platter and serve as a side salad.

Per serving: 72 cals, 5.8g fat, 0.9g sat fat, 2.8g total sugars, 0.2g salt

Did you know...?
80% of Sainsbury's total tomato sales are UK sourced, when in season

Stacked BLT salad

Grill 8 slices of streaky bacon until crispy. Cut 4 large vine tomatoes into ¼ in-thick slices. Lay on a plate in a single layer and season with salt and freshly ground black pepper. Halve, stone and peel 1 avocado, then slice each half into 8 pieces lengthways. Create 4 BLT stacks by layering the tomatoes with alternate bacon and avocado, adding a few rocket leaves. Sprinkle with olive oil and extra black pepper. Great with lightly toasted bread.

SERVES 4 Prep time: 5 minutes Cook time: 10 minutes

Per serving: 196 cals, 16g fat, 3.6g sat fat, 1.6g total sugars, 1.1g salt

'This refreshing side salad is great with grilled meat or fish'

Serves 4
Prep time: 5 minutes
Cook time: 25 minutes

Bacon, asparagus & poached egg salad

Choose the freshest eggs you can find for this salad, as they will hold their shape well during poaching

1 x 240g pack Taste the Difference dry-cure streaky bacon, cut into 2cm pieces
2 x 100g packs Sainsbury's asparagus tips, trimmed
4 medium eggs
1 x 70g bag Sainsbury's wild rocket

FOR THE DRESSING
1 tablespoon red wine vinegar
2 tablespoons extra virgin olive oil
1 shallot, peeled and finely chopped
pinch of sugar

1   Heat a non-stick frying pan over a medium heat and dry-fry the bacon until crispy. Remove with a slotted spoon and set aside. Add the asparagus to the pan and cook for 4 minutes, turning frequently.

2   Meanwhile, bring a large pan of water to the boil. Turn off the heat. Break an egg into a cup and gently lower it into the water. Repeat with another egg, then put a lid on the pan and poach for 3-4 minutes. Scoop out with a slotted spoon. Bring the water back to boiling, then turn off the heat and repeat with the remaining 2 eggs.

3   In a bowl, mix together the ingredients for the dressing. Place the bacon, asparagus and rocket in a large bowl and toss with the dressing. Divide between 4 plates, topping each one with an egg and seasoning with freshly ground black pepper. Great served with crusty bread.

Per serving: 406 cals, 31.9g fat, 12g sat fat, 1.4g total sugars, 3.2g salt

Did you know...?
Sainsbury's was the first major supermarket to source all its whole eggs from cage-free hens, improving the lives of 800,000 birds

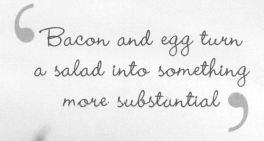

Serves 4
Prep time: 15 minutes,
plus marinating time
Cook time: 10 minutes

Rocket & chilli squid salad

If you've never cooked squid before, this recipe is your ideal introduction. By scoring it in a crisscross pattern, it will curl up attractively during cooking

2 stalks lemon grass, peeled and very finely chopped
3 cloves garlic, peeled and finely chopped
2 tablespoons caster sugar
2 red chillies, deseeded and finely chopped
zest and juice of 2 limes

3 tablespoons sunflower oil
600g cleaned fresh squid
2 x 70g bags Sainsbury's wild rocket
1 bunch spring onions, trimmed, halved and shredded into 4cm lengths
½ x 80g bag Sainsbury's prawn crackers

1 Preheat the oven to 120°C, fan 100°C, gas ½.

2 To make the dressing, use a pestle and mortar to pound the lemon grass, garlic and sugar to a paste. Stir in the chilli, lime zest, lime juice and 2 tablespoons oil. Season with salt and freshly ground black pepper.

3 Cut the squid into 4cm pieces and, using a sharp knife, score the skin lightly in a crisscross pattern. Place in a non-metallic bowl and pour over the dressing. Marinate in the fridge for 15 minutes.

4 Heat a wok or large frying pan until searing hot, then add the remaining 1 tablespoon oil and swirl around the pan. Lift the squid from the marinade and add to the pan. Stir-fry in 2 batches for 3 minutes each, until cooked through and lightly charred. Set aside and keep warm in the oven.

5 Add the marinade to the hot pan and let it bubble for 3-4 minutes, until thickened. Divide the rocket and spring onions between 4 shallow bowls. Top with the squid and spoon over the marinade. Serve with the prawn crackers.

Per serving: 313 cals, 14.4g fat, 2.5g sat fat, 12.4g total sugars, 0.7g salt

‘The peppery flavours of rocket, onion and chilli are great with squid’

Serves 4
Prep time: 15 minutes
Cook time: 15 minutes,
plus resting time

Lamb & bulgar wheat salad

The traditional partnership of lamb and mint is given an exciting new twist in this delicious bulgar wheat salad

200g bulgar wheat

400g lamb neck fillet

2 tablespoons olive oil

2 x 250g packs Taste the Difference vine tomatoes, roughly chopped

½ x cucumber, roughly chopped

1 x 28g pack Sainsbury's fresh mint, leaves picked and roughly chopped

1 x 28g pack Sainsbury's fresh flat-leaf parsley, leaves picked and roughly chopped

2 tablespoons mint sauce

seeds of 1 pomegranate

1 Place the bulgar wheat in a bowl and just cover with boiling water. Cover and set aside for 15 minutes to soften and absorb the liquid.

2 Meanwhile, heat a griddle pan or grill to hot. Rub the lamb with 1 tablespoon oil and season with salt and freshly ground black pepper. Cook on the griddle, or place on a foil-lined baking tray and cook under the grill, turning the heat down to medium. Cook for 5-6 minutes on each side, then remove and set aside to rest for 10 minutes.

3 Meanwhile, drain the bulgar wheat and toss with the tomatoes, cucumber, mint and parsley. Stir through the mint sauce and the remaining 1 tablespoon oil.

4 Slice the lamb. Serve the salad on a large platter topped with the lamb and sprinkled with the pomegranate seeds, and let everyone help themselves.

Per serving: 345 cals, 14.3g fat, 4g sat fat, 15g total sugars, 0.6g salt

"Jewel-like pomegranate seeds give this salad extra appeal"

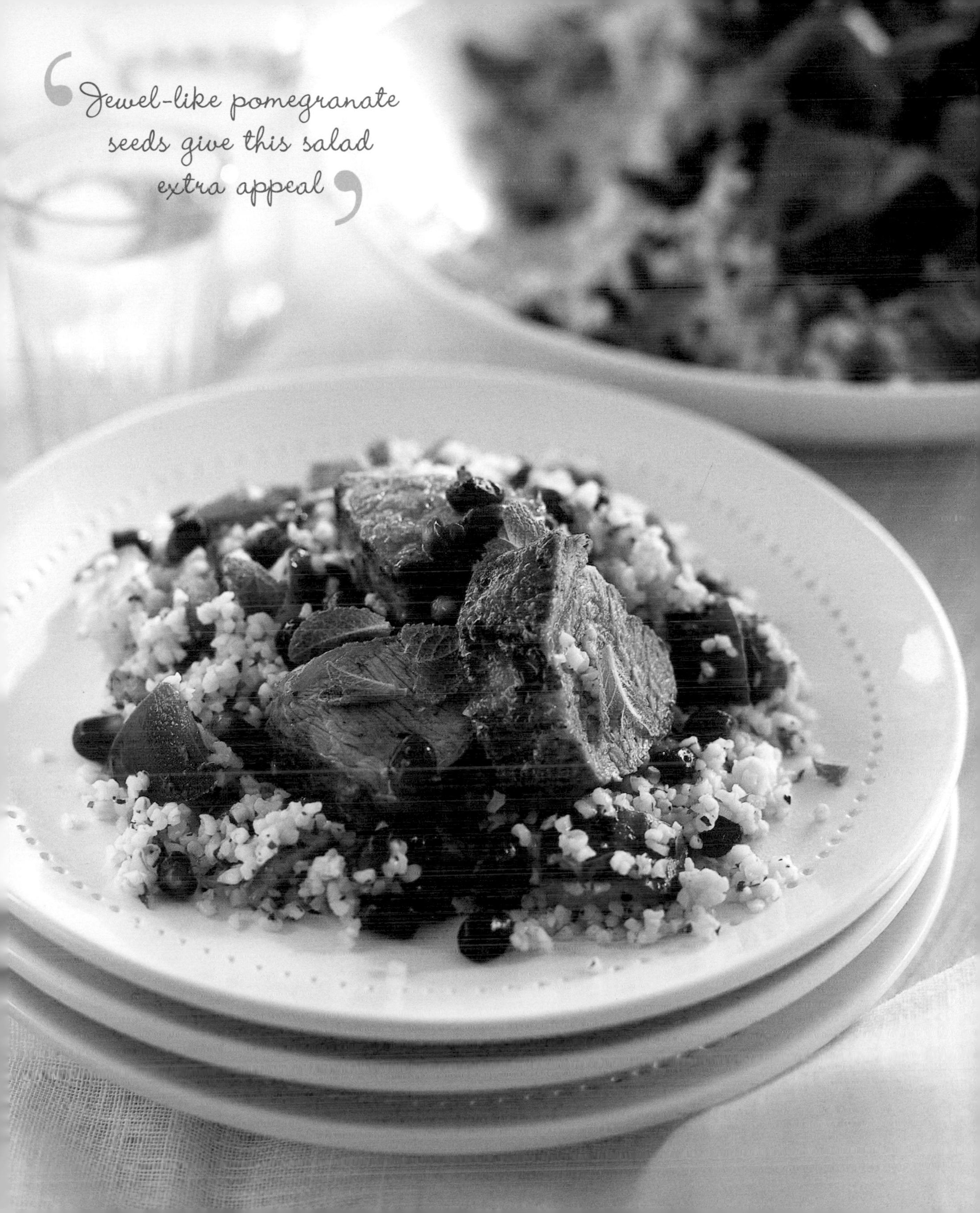

summer dinners

Broad bean & pea risotto · 54

Noodles with roast chicken, chilli & watercress · 56

Roast leg of lamb with turnips & shallots · 58

Zesty spring vegetables · 58

Cheese & thyme stuffed mushrooms · 60

Paella · 62

Roast tomato & pesto tagliatelle · 62

Mexican-style meatball wraps · 64

Sesame chicken & pepper stir-fry · 66

Goats' cheese frittata · 68

Two-pea pasta · 70

Tuna with linguine & olives · 70

Smoky beef tacos · 72

Pasta alla Norma · 74

Pea & potato gnocchi with fried sage · 76

Prosciutto, basil & mozzarella pizzas · 78

Vietnamese chilli noodles · 80

Serves 2
Prep time: 25 minutes
Cook time: 35 minutes

Broad bean & pea risotto

Risotto isn't as labour-intensive as you might believe – and the results are fantastic. This classic recipe uses tasty summer veg

150g fresh or frozen broad beans

75g fresh or frozen peas

1 x 500g pouch Sainsbury's Signature vegetable stock

25g unsalted butter

2 cloves garlic, peeled and finely chopped

½ x bunch spring onions, finely chopped

110g Arborio rice

60ml white wine

15g parmesan, finely grated

1   Blanch the broad beans and peas in boiling water for 2 minutes (if you're using frozen beans and peas, they will only need 30 seconds to 1 minute). Drain, refresh in cold water and drain again. Slip the beans out of their skins, then set the beans and peas aside.

2   In a large saucepan, heat the vegetable stock to simmering point, then keep warm over a low heat.

3   In another saucepan, melt the butter over a medium-high heat, then add the garlic and spring onions and sauté until soft. Add the rice and stir until all the grains are coated in butter. Stir for 2 minutes, until it looks translucent.

4   Pour in the white wine, stirring. Once it has been almost absorbed, stir in a ladleful of the hot stock. Continue like this, adding the stock a ladleful at a time, for 20-25 minutes, until the rice is creamy and al dente.

5   When the stock is absorbed, stir in the peas and broad beans. Season with salt and freshly ground black pepper, and garnish with the parmesan to serve.

Per serving: 409 cals, 14.4g fat, 9.8g sat fat, 2.8g total sugars, 0.1g salt

Deliciously creamy risotto is a classic Italian dish

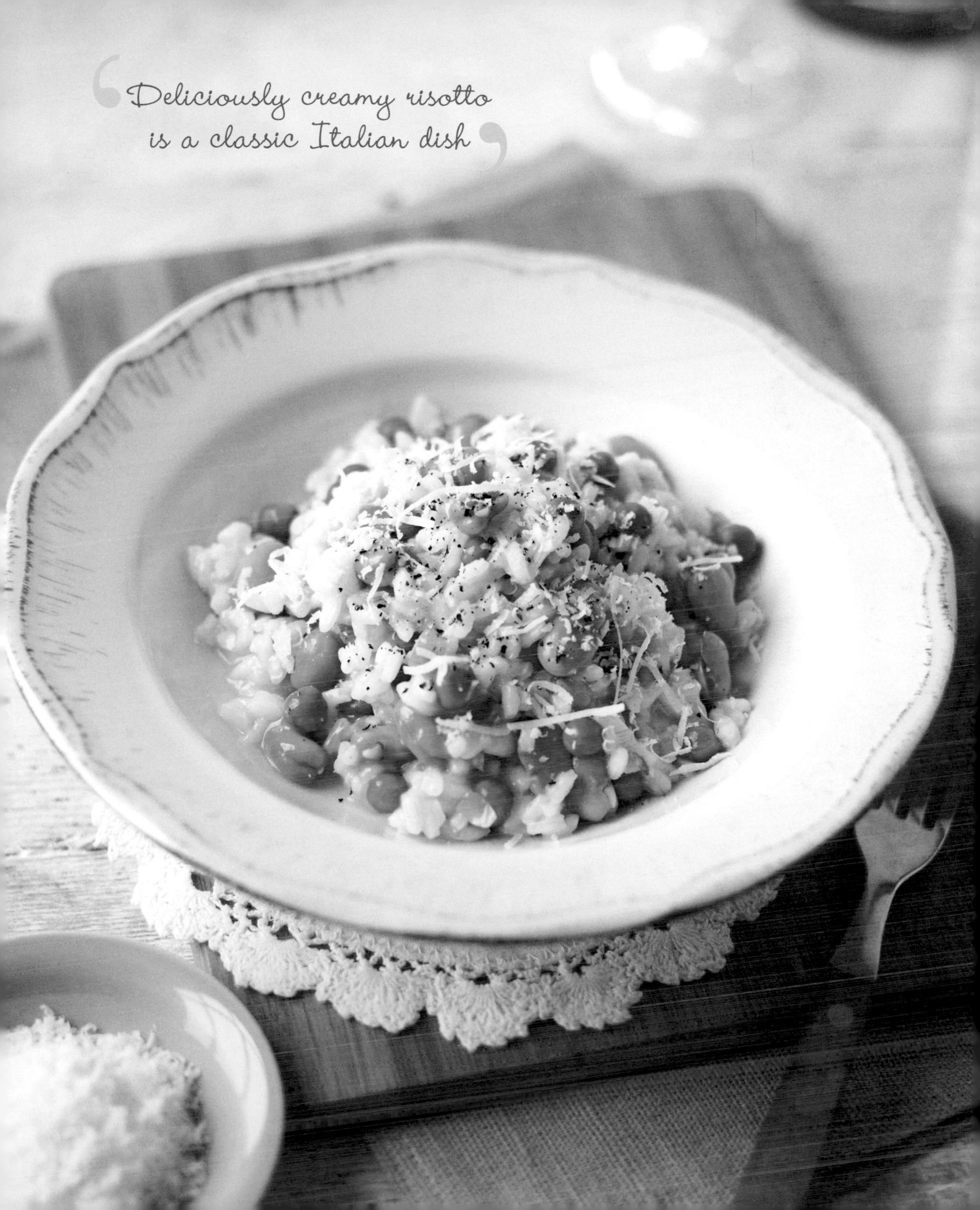

Serves 4
Prep time: 5 minutes
Cook time: 10 minutes

Noodles with roast chicken, chilli & watercress

This quick and easy dish is a great way to use up any leftovers from your Sunday roast, as it also works well with beef or pork

400g leftover roast chicken
2 tablespoons toasted sesame oil
1 red chilli, deseeded and finely sliced
2 tablespoons sesame seeds

2 x 410g packs Sainsbury's free-range fresh egg noodles
1 x 75g pack Sainsbury's watercress

1   Remove any skin or fat from your leftover meat and tear or slice it into strips.

2   Heat the oil in a wok or large frying pan, then add the chilli. Cook for 1 minute, then add the meat and sesame seeds. Cook for 2-3 minutes, until heated through.

3   Add the noodles and stir through. Stir-fry for 3-4 minutes.

4   Remove from the heat and stir through the watercress before serving.

Per serving: 612 cals, 23.5g fat, 3.4g sat fat, 1.1g total sugars, 0.2g salt

'A tasty way to use up leftovers from your Sunday roast'

Serves 6
Prep time: 20 minutes
Cook time: 1½ hours, plus resting time

Roast leg of lamb

with turnips & shallots

This delicious recipe for roast lamb is so easy - once it's all in the oven you can forget about it until it's cooked. Try serving it with the zesty spring vegetables

1 x 2kg whole lamb leg, bone in	8 turnips, peeled and quartered
1 tablespoon olive oil	1 head garlic, cloves separated but unpeeled
1 x 400g pack Sainsbury's shallots, peeled	½ x 15g pack Sainsbury's fresh thyme

1 Preheat the oven to 190°C, fan 170°C, gas 5.

2 Rub the lamb with the olive oil and season well with freshly ground black pepper and lightly with salt. Place in a large roasting tin and surround with the shallots, turnips and garlic cloves. Scatter over the thyme and cover with foil. Roast for 1 hour, 15 minutes for rare meat, or 1 hour, 30 minutes for medium.

3 Once cooked, wrap in foil and leave to rest for 10-20 minutes, then carve and serve with zesty spring vegetables (see recipe below).

Per serving: 705 cals, 43.5g fat, 18.3g sat fat, 8.9g total sugars, trace salt

Zesty spring vegetables

Boil 100g fresh broad beans for 4-5 minutes (or frozen broad beans for 1-2 minutes), until tender, then drain. When cool enough to handle, peel the skins off. Steam 350g asparagus, trimmed, and 2 courgettes, sliced, for 3-4 minutes, adding 50g fresh or frozen peas for the final 2 minutes. Drain. Toss with the beans to warm through. Season. Sprinkle over the zest and juice of 1 lemon and 25g toasted flaked almonds.

SERVES 6
Prep time: 10 minutes Cook time: 10 minutes
Per serving: 67 cals, 3.1g fat, nil sat fat, 2.3g total sugars, trace salt

Melt-in-the-mouth
roast lamb is a
family favourite

Serves 4
Prep time: 10 minutes
Cook time: 20 minutes

Cheese & thyme stuffed mushrooms

with pesto-houmous potatoes

These herby stuffed mushrooms can be cooked under the grill or on the barbecue for a delicious summer supper

1kg new potatoes, halved
1 x 200g pot Sainsbury's pesto-topped houmous
1 bunch spring onions, sliced
8 portabella mushrooms, stems removed

2 x 125g packs Sainsbury's Abergavenny soft goats' cheese, chopped
2 tablespoons fresh thyme leaves, chopped
1 clove garlic, peeled and crushed

1 Place the potatoes in a pan of cold water and bring to the boil. Cook for 10-15 minutes, until tender, then drain and toss with the pesto houmous and spring onions.

2 Meanwhile, place the mushrooms on a double layer of foil and season with freshly ground black pepper. Preheat the grill to medium-high.

3 Mix together the goats' cheese, thyme and garlic, and spoon over the mushrooms. Grill for 10-15 minutes. Alternatively, you can cook these on a hot barbecue for 10 minutes. Serve, two per person, with the potatoes.

Per serving: 561 cals, 30.6g fat, 15.4g sat fat, 4.3g total sugars, 1.1g salt

Tip
Instead of using the pesto-topped houmous, you could stir 2 tablespoons pesto into 150g houmous

Serves 4
Prep time: 10 minutes
Cook time: 35 minutes

45 mins

Paella

This summery Spanish favourite, made with spicy chorizo, sweet smoked paprika and a selection of seafood, is great for sharing

1 tablespoon olive oil
1 red onion, peeled and chopped
1 red pepper, deseeded and chopped
½ x 250g pack Sainsbury's mini cooking chorizo, sliced
350g Sainsbury's Spanish paella rice

1 teaspoon La Chinata sweet smoked paprika
a pinch of saffron
800g Sainsbury's Signature vegetable or chicken stock
1 x 235g pack Sainsbury's seafood selection
1 tablespoon fresh flat-leaf parsley, chopped

1 Heat the oil in a large pan, then add the onion and fry for 5 minutes. Add the pepper and chorizo and cook until the chorizo is crispy.

2 Stir in the paella rice, smoked paprika and saffron, and heat through. Add the stock, bring to the boil, then simmer for 15 minutes, until almost all the liquid is absorbed.

3 Add the seafood mix. Season with salt and freshly ground black pepper and cook for 5 minutes. Serve sprinkled with the parsley.

Per serving: 557 cals, 17g fat, 4.5g sat fat, 5.4g total sugars, 2.2g salt

Roast tomato & pesto tagliatelle

Preheat the oven to 220°C, fan 200°C, gas 7. Place 1 x 270g pack Taste the Difference vittoria tomatoes, halved, on a baking tray. Add 2 cloves garlic, peeled and sliced, and toss with 1 tablespoon olive oil. Roast for 10 minutes. Meanwhile, cook 500g fresh egg tagliatelle following pack instructions, then drain. Stir in the tomatoes and garlic, 75g green pesto and 25g finely grated parmesan. Serve topped with basil leaves and parmesan shavings.

SERVES 4 Prep time: 10 minutes Cook time: 15 minutes

45 mins

Per serving: 356 cals, 16g fat, 4.6g sat fat, 2.4g total sugars, 1g salt

Serves 6
Prep time: 20 minutes,
plus chilling time
Cook time: 30 minutes

Mexican-style meatball wraps

Full of colour and flavour, these Mexican meatballs are great for tucking into with friends on a relaxed summer evening

---

2 tablespoons tomato purée
1 teaspoon ground cumin
1 teaspoon mild chilli powder
1 x 500g pack Sainsbury's lean steak mince
50g white breadcrumbs
1 red onion, peeled and finely sliced
1 red pepper, deseeded and sliced
1 x 420g tin Sainsbury's red kidney beans in chilli sauce

1 x 198g tin Sainsbury's sweetcorn, drained
1 x 6-pack Sainsbury's be good to yourself tortilla wraps
1 tablespoon olive oil, for brushing
6 tablespoons natural yogurt
½ x 28g pack Sainsbury's fresh coriander, leaves only
paprika, to serve
lime wedges, to serve

---

1 In a bowl, mix together the tomato purée, cumin, chilli powder, mince and breadcrumbs and season well with salt and freshly ground black pepper. Roll the mixture into 18 meatballs and chill in the fridge for 5 minutes.

2 Heat a large, non-stick frying pan until hot, then add the meatballs and fry over a medium heat, rotating every 1-2 minutes, for about 10 minutes, until browned all over. Add the onion and pepper and fry for a further 5 minutes. Stir in the beans and sweetcorn and continue to cook for a further 5-10 minutes, until the meatballs are cooked through.

3 Heat another frying pan until hot. Brush each tortilla wrap with a little olive oil, then fry in the hot pan for 30 seconds on each side. Top each wrap with 3 meatballs and some pepper and bean mixture, then add yogurt and coriander leaves. Sprinkle with paprika and serve with lime wedges.

Per serving: 363 cals, 13.3g fat, 6.2g sat fat, 11g total sugars, 1g salt

Serves 2
Prep time: 15 minutes
Cook time: 20 minutes

Sesame chicken & pepper stir-fry

The toasty taste of sesame adds a nutty touch to this oriental stir-fry

1 tablespoon cornflour

150g Sainsbury's Signature fresh chicken stock

1 tablespoon light soy sauce

½ tablespoon olive oil

½ x 400g pack Sainsbury's mini chicken fillets, cut into pieces

1 clove garlic, peeled and finely sliced

½ x bunch spring onions, finely sliced

2 small peppers, preferably different colours, deseeded and cut into strips

½ tablespoon sesame oil

1 tablespoon sesame seeds

1 x 250g pack Sainsbury's 2 minute meals long grain rice

1   Place the cornflour in a bowl and whisk in the stock and soy sauce to a smooth consistency. Set aside.

2   In a large wok, heat the olive oil and fry the chicken pieces, garlic and half the spring onions until the chicken is just cooked through. Add the peppers and cook, stirring, for a further 5 minutes, then add the sauce. Cook for a further 5 minutes, until the sauce has thickened slightly.

3   Stir in the remaining spring onions, then drizzle with the sesame oil and sprinkle with the sesame seeds.

4   Meanwhile, microwave the rice following pack instructions, and serve with the chicken.

Per serving: 549 cals, 15.4g fat, 3g sat fat, 11.3g total sugars, 1.9g salt

"Vibrant vegetables help this stir-fry look good and taste even better"

Serves 4
Prep time: 10 minutes
Cook time: 15 minutes

Goats' cheese frittata

This quick and tasty frittata is ideal for those days when you'd rather be out enjoying the weather than be stuck in the kitchen

1 tablespoon olive oil
4 Sainsbury's medium Woodland free-range eggs
1 x 100g pack Sainsbury's Somerset goats' cheese, chopped

12 Taste the Difference SunBlush® tomatoes, chopped
1–2 tablespoons fresh flat-leaf parsley, chopped

1 Preheat the grill to medium.

2 Heat the oil in a non-stick 18cm frying pan. Meanwhile, beat the eggs with 1 tablespoon water and a little salt and freshly ground black pepper. Pour into the pan and cook for 5 minutes, or until golden underneath.

3 Sprinkle on the cheese and SunBlush tomatoes, then grill for about 10 minutes, until just set. Serve cut into wedges, garnished with parsley.

Per serving: 239 cals, 19.5g fat, 2.3g sat fat, 2.6g total sugars, 0.7g salt

Did you know...?
Sainsbury's was the first major supermarket to source all its whole eggs from cage-free hens, improving the lives of 800,000 birds

Serves 2
Prep time: 10 minutes
Cook time: 10 minutes

Two-pea pasta

Fresh tarragon and lemon add extra flavour to this simple veggie pasta

100ml crème fraîche

zest and juice of 1 lemon

½ tablespoon chopped fresh tarragon

½ x 500g pack Sainsbury's fresh penne pasta

100g frozen peas

½ x 200g pack Sainsbury's sugar snap peas

1 Place the crème fraîche in a bowl. Stir in the lemon zest, lemon juice and tarragon, then set aside.

2 Cook the pasta following pack instructions, adding the frozen peas and sugar snaps for the final minute of cooking.

3 Drain the pasta and vegetables, reserving a little of the cooking water. Return the pasta and vegetables to the pan, add the crème fraîche mixture and stir through. Adjust the consistency with the reserved cooking water, if necessary. Season with salt and freshly ground black pepper and serve.

Per serving: 318 cals, 7.6g fat, 2.9g sat fat, 5.2g total sugars, 0.5g salt

Tip for meat eaters
Grill a few rashers of smoked streaky bacon. Allow to cool, then crumble over each serving at the end for an extra flavour boost

Tuna with linguine & olives

Cook 300g linguine following pack instructions. Meanwhile, fry 1 peeled and crushed clove garlic in 1 tablespoon olive oil for 1 minute. Add 250g cherry tomatoes, halved and deseeded, and cook for 3 minutes. Drain the pasta. Toss through the tomatoes, 3 tablespoons olive oil, the juice of 1 lemon, 1 x 28g pack Sainsbury's flat-leaf parsley, chopped, 75g pitted green olives, chopped, and 1 x 200g tin tuna in sunflower oil, drained and flaked. Season and serve.

SERVES 4 Prep time: 15 minutes Cook time: 10 minutes

Per serving: 489 cals, 18.7g fat, 2.2g sat fat, 5g total sugars, 1.5g salt

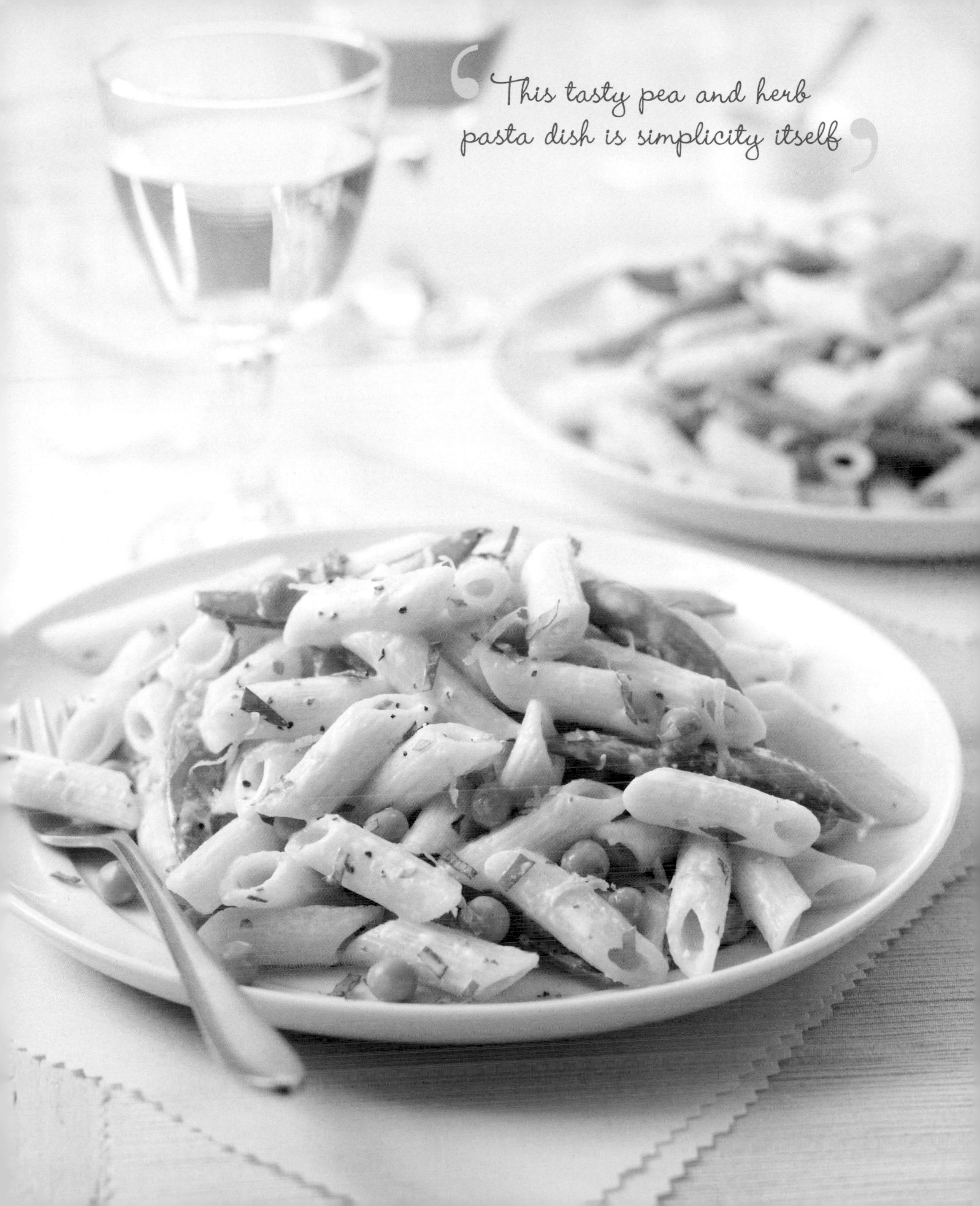

"This tasty pea and herb pasta dish is simplicity itself"

Serves 4
Prep time: 20 minutes
Cook time: 30 minutes

Smoky beef tacos

This easy meal is the perfect way to end a day of summer family fun - the kids will love to pile in their own filling and toppings

1 tablespoon olive oil
1 red onion, peeled and chopped
1 x 500g pack Sainsbury's lean beef steak mince
½ tablespoon chilli powder
1 green pepper, deseeded and chopped
100g Sainsbury's barbecue sauce

1 x 390g carton Sainsbury's SO organic black beans, drained
4 taco shells
1 iceberg lettuce, shredded
50g Cheddar, grated
soured cream, to serve

1 Heat the oil in a large frying pan. Add the onion and fry until translucent. Add the mince and chilli powder and cook until it begins to caramelise.

2 Stir in the pepper and continue to fry for a further 5 minutes. Add the barbecue sauce and black beans. Simmer for 10 minutes.

3 Fill the tacos with the lettuce. Add the beef mixture and sprinkle on the cheese. Serve with soured cream to drizzle over.

Per serving: 533 cals, 30.8g fat, 15.5g sat fat, 11.4g total sugars, 0.5g salt

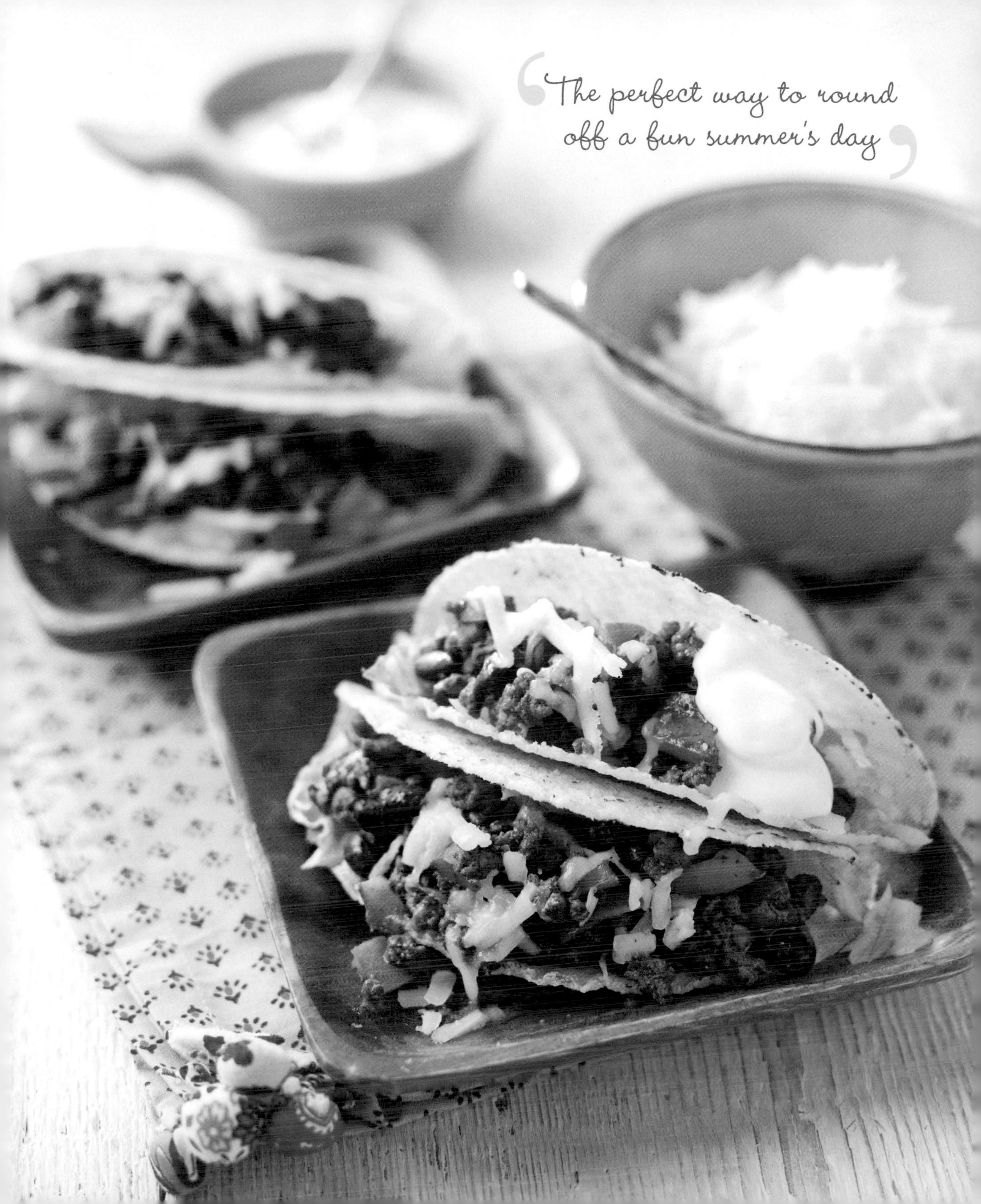

"The perfect way to round off a fun summer's day"

Serves 4
Prep time: 15 minutes
Cook time: 30 minutes

Pasta alla Norma

This aromatic dish was named in honour of the opera *Norma* by Sicilian composer Vincenzo Bellini, who was an avid fan of the recipe

2 tablespoons olive oil	1 x 700g jar Sainsbury's Italian passata sauce
2 aubergines, cubed	320g spaghetti
1 onion, peeled and chopped	handful of basil leaves, torn
2 cloves garlic, peeled and chopped	100g ricotta cheese

1 Heat 1 tablespoon oil in a large pan and fry the aubergine cubes until golden on all sides. (Alternatively, place on a roasting tray, drizzle with the oil and cook in the oven at 200°C, fan 180°C, gas 6 for 20-25 minutes, or until golden.) Remove from the pan and set aside.

2 Add the remaining 1 tablespoon oil to the pan. Cook the onion for 3-4 minutes, then add the garlic and stir through for 1-2 minutes. Pour in the jar of passata and bring to the boil, then turn down the heat and stir in the cooked aubergine. Season well with salt and freshly ground black pepper and cook for a further 6-8 minutes.

3 Meanwhile, bring a large pan of salted water to the boil and cook the spaghetti following pack instructions.

4 Drain the pasta and toss through the sauce along with the basil. Spoon over the ricotta and serve immediately.

Per serving: 465 cals, 10.3g fat, 4.9g sat fat, 17.5g total sugars, 1g salt

'This simple pasta dish is full of enticing Italian flavours'

Serves 4
Prep time: 20 minutes
Cook time: 35 minutes

Pea & potato gnocchi

with fried sage

Try something new with potatoes – have a go at our easy gnocchi, flavoured with pea and mint and served with a wonderful sage butter

500g Maris Piper or King Edward potatoes (must be evenly sized)
100g fresh peas, podded
½ x 28g pack Sainsbury's fresh mint, leaves finely chopped
100g 00 grade flour, plus extra for dusting

1 medium egg white
2 tablespoons olive oil
½ x 20g pack Sainsbury's fresh sage, leaves picked
½ x 50g bag Sainsbury's pea shoots, to serve

1 Place the potatoes, whole and with their skins on, in a pan of cold water. Bring to the boil and cook for 30 minutes, until just tender. Drain and leave to cool slightly. Holding the potatoes in a clean tea towel, peel off the skins, then place in a ricer or stir through a sieve.

2 Meanwhile, cook the peas in a small pan of boiling water for 4–5 minutes, until tender. Drain, place in a food processor and purée until smooth.

3 Place the mint in a bowl with the flour, egg white, potato and pea purée. Season with salt and freshly ground black pepper. Mix very thoroughly and knead for a few minutes, until smooth. Divide the mixture into 2 or 3 pieces, then roll on a floured surface into sausages about 2.5cm in diameter. Cut each sausage into 3cm pieces, pressing each one lightly with a fork.

4 Bring a large, shallow pan of water to the boil. Drop in the gnocchi (this can be done in batches) and cook for 2–3 minutes, or until they rise to the surface. Divide between 4 plates.

5 Heat the oil in a shallow pan, then add the sage leaves and cook for 1–2 minutes. Remove the sage leaves and place on kitchen paper to remove any excess oil. Serve the gnocchi with the fried sage and pea shoots.

Per serving: 291 cals, 9.1g fat, 4.2g sat fat, 1.7g total sugars, trace salt

'The fried sage is perfect with these little Italian potato dumplings'

Serves 6
(3 x 25cm pizzas)
Prep time: 30 minutes,
plus rising time
Cook time: 45 minutes

Prosciutto, basil & mozzarella pizzas

These homemade pizzas will be a hit with the adults and kids alike

FOR THE PIZZA DOUGH BASE
1 x 7g sachet Sainsbury's fast action dried yeast
300ml warm water
1 teaspoon sugar
450g strong plain flour, plus extra for dusting
50g semolina

FOR THE SAUCE AND TOPPING
1 tablespoon olive oil, plus extra for drizzling

1 onion, peeled and finely diced
2 cloves garlic, peeled and crushed
1 x 700g jar Sainsbury's passata
1 teaspoon dried Italian herb seasoning
2 x 150g packs Sainsbury's mozzarella, torn
2 x 70g packs Sainsbury's prosciutto crudo slices, torn
12 cherry tomatoes, halved
½ x 28g pack Sainsbury's fresh basil, leaves picked

1 To make the pizza dough, mix together the yeast, water and sugar in a jug until dissolved, then leave until frothy.

2 Place the flour and semolina in a bowl, then slowly add the yeasty liquid and mix into a dough. Tip the dough onto a lightly floured surface and knead for 5 minutes, until smooth and elastic. Shape the dough into a ball, then rest in a warm place, covered with a clean tea towel, until doubled in size (this should take about 45 minutes).

3 Meanwhile, make the sauce. Heat the oil in a frying pan over a medium heat, then add the onion and garlic and cook gently until the onion has softened. Add the passata and dried herbs, and simmer for 10-15 minutes, stirring frequently. Preheat the oven to 220°C, fan 200°C, gas 7.

4 Divide the dough into 3, then roll out each piece to make 3 x 25cm pizza bases. Place on lightly floured pizza trays and spread each with sauce.

5 Scatter over the mozzarella and top with the prosciutto and tomatoes. Drizzle with olive oil, if you like. Bake for 10-15 minutes, or until golden brown. Scatter on the basil leaves, then serve.

Per serving: 559 cals, 17.8g fat, 11.2g sat fat, 10g total sugars, 1.9g salt

Serves 4
Prep time: 15 minutes
Cook time: 10 minutes

Vietnamese chilli noodles

Lemon grass, chilli and lime give these noodles real zing

1 x 300g pack Sharwood's Thai style ribbon noodles
½ x stalk lemon grass, roughly chopped
1 clove garlic, peeled and crushed
1 small fat red chilli, deseeded and finely chopped
2 tablespoons light soy sauce
zest and juice of 1 small lime, plus extra lime wedges, to serve
1 tablespoon Sainsbury's groundnut oil

1 x 175g pack Sainsbury's baby corn, halved lengthways
2 red peppers, deseeded and cut into thin strips
1 x 200g pack Sainsbury's sugar snap peas, shredded
75g beansprouts
25g salted peanuts, roughly chopped
1 x 28g pack Sainsbury's fresh coriander, chopped

1 Microwave the noodles following pack instructions, then tip into a large bowl.

2 Using a pestle and mortar, pound the lemon grass, garlic and chilli to a paste. Stir in the soy sauce, lime zest, lime juice and ½ tablespoon groundnut oil.

3 Heat the remaining ½ tablespoon oil in a large wok or frying pan and stir-fry the baby corn, peppers and sugar snap peas for 3-4 minutes, until lightly charred. Add to the noodles, then stir in the chilli mixture, beansprouts, peanuts and half the coriander. Toss until well combined. Scatter with the remaining coriander and serve with lime wedges.

Per serving: 280 cals, 8.9g fat, 1g sat fat, 9.4g sugar, 1.4g salt

"Tangy and fiery, these chilli noodles pack quite a punch"

fish & seafood

Pan-fried cod with lemon, olives & parsley 84

Rustic fish bake 86

Herb-crusted roast salmon with mash & vine tomatoes 88

Zesty haddock parcels 90

Oriental stir-fried prawns 92

Fish & chips with tartare sauce & mushy peas 94

Coconut fish curry 96

Pan-fried lime & chilli scallops 98

Roast monkfish with cherry tomatoes & red onion 100

Herby fish fingers 102

Seared tuna with salsa verde & new potatoes 104

Soy & citrus salmon salad 106

Griddled sea bass with minty green salad 108

King prawn bake & linguine 110

Salmon & red onion fishcakes with dill & garlic mayo 112

Pan-fried sea bream with pineapple salsa 114

Serves 4
Prep time: 10 minutes
Cook time: 10 minutes

Pan-fried cod

with lemon, olives & parsley

A topping of crunchy pine nuts, zesty lemon and tangy olives is the perfect complement to pan-fried cod

---

4 tablespoons plain flour
4 Sainsbury's skinless cod fillets, each about 175g
50g butter
zest and juice of 1 lemon
6 pitted black olives, roughly chopped

2 tablespoons toasted pine nuts
½ x 28g pack Sainsbury's fresh flat-leaf parsley, chopped
1 x 300g pack Sainsbury's dwarf beans, to serve

---

1 Tip the flour onto a plate and season with salt and freshly ground black pepper, then coat the fish on both sides.

2 Melt the butter in a large, non-stick, lidded frying pan. When bubbling, add the fish and cook over a medium heat until the underside is cooked and browned (this will take about 4–5 minutes). Carefully turn the fish over and turn down the heat to low.

3 Scatter over the lemon zest, olives, pine nuts and most of the parsley, and drizzle over the lemon juice. Season with salt and freshly ground black pepper. Cover the pan and cook for 2–4 minutes, until the fish is cooked through and has started to flake. Scatter with the remaining parsley.

4 Meanwhile, place the dwarf beans in a pan of boiling water and cook for 4–5 minutes, until tender. Drain and serve with the cod.

Per serving: 388 cals, 18g fat, 7.5g sat fat, 2.5g total sugars, 0.3g salt

Fair on fish
Sainsbury's sources all fresh and frozen cod from MSC-certified line-caught fisheries in Alaska and Norway, and from a well-managed Icelandic line-caught fishery

Serves 4
Prep time: 10 minutes
Cook time: 50 minutes

Rustic fish bake

Layers of roasted vegetables are topped with juicy white fish and herbs in this rustic bake. Here we've used cod, but sea bass or pollock work equally well

2 large potatoes, peeled and cut into 1cm thick slices
5 tablespoons olive oil
2 courgettes, cut into 1cm thick slices
300g tomatoes, cut into 1cm thick slices
4 tablespoons Sainsbury's red pesto

2 cloves garlic, peeled and finely chopped
4 thick skinless cod loins
½ x 28g pack Sainsbury's fresh flat-leaf parsley, to serve
lemon wedges, to serve

1 Preheat the oven to 180°C, fan 160°C, gas 4. Arrange the potatoes in a baking dish. Drizzle with 1 tablespoon oil and bake for 15 minutes, until just tender.

2 Add the courgette and tomato to the baking dish, interspersing them with the potato slices.

3 In a small jug, mix together the pesto, garlic and the remaining 4 tablespoons oil, then drizzle over the vegetables. Season with freshly ground black pepper, then bake for another 20 minutes.

4 Season the fish with salt and freshly ground black pepper, then lay the loins on top of the vegetables. Drizzle with some oil from the baking dish and return to the oven for a further 10-15 minutes, until the cod is cooked through. Serve sprinkled with parsley, with lemon wedges on the side.

Per serving: 292 cals, 20.1g fat, 3g sat fat, 4.9g total sugars, 0.6g salt

Fair on fish
Sainsbury's is proud to be the largest UK retailer of MSC-certified sustainable fish and seafood products, with over 80 products which carry the MSC ecolabel

"Roasted Mediterranean vegetables complement white fish beautifully"

Herb-crusted roast salmon

with mash & vine tomatoes

Transform salmon fillets with this fabulous crumb topping infused with fresh rosemary and thyme

1kg Maris Piper potatoes, peeled and cut into small pieces
25g unsalted butter
100ml semi-skimmed milk
2 x 270g packs Sainsbury's vittoria tomatoes
1 tablespoon olive oil, plus extra for greasing
75g fresh breadcrumbs
2 sprigs fresh rosemary, leaves picked and chopped

4 sprigs fresh thyme, leaves picked and chopped
zest of 1 lemon and the juice of $\frac{1}{2}$
4 x 120g salmon fillets, skin on, from the fish counter
1 x 300g tub Taste the Difference watercress sauce

1   Preheat the oven to 200°C, fan 180°C, gas 6.

2   Place the potatoes in a pan of cold water and bring to the boil. Simmer for 15 minutes until tender, then drain and mash with the butter and milk.

3   Meanwhile, place the tomatoes on a baking tray and drizzle over the olive oil. Bake in the oven for 15-20 minutes.

4   Meanwhile, place the breadcrumbs, rosemary, thyme, lemon zest and lemon juice in a food processor and whizz. Place the salmon fillets on another lightly oiled baking tray and top with the herb and lemon breadcrumb mixture. Bake for 10-12 minutes, until cooked through.

5   Heat the watercress sauce in the microwave, following pack instructions. Serve with the salmon, mashed potato and roasted tomatoes.

Per serving: 657 cals, 29g fat, 10.8g sat fat, 9.6g total sugars, 1.2g salt

'A herby breadcrumb topping gives salmon an exciting twist'

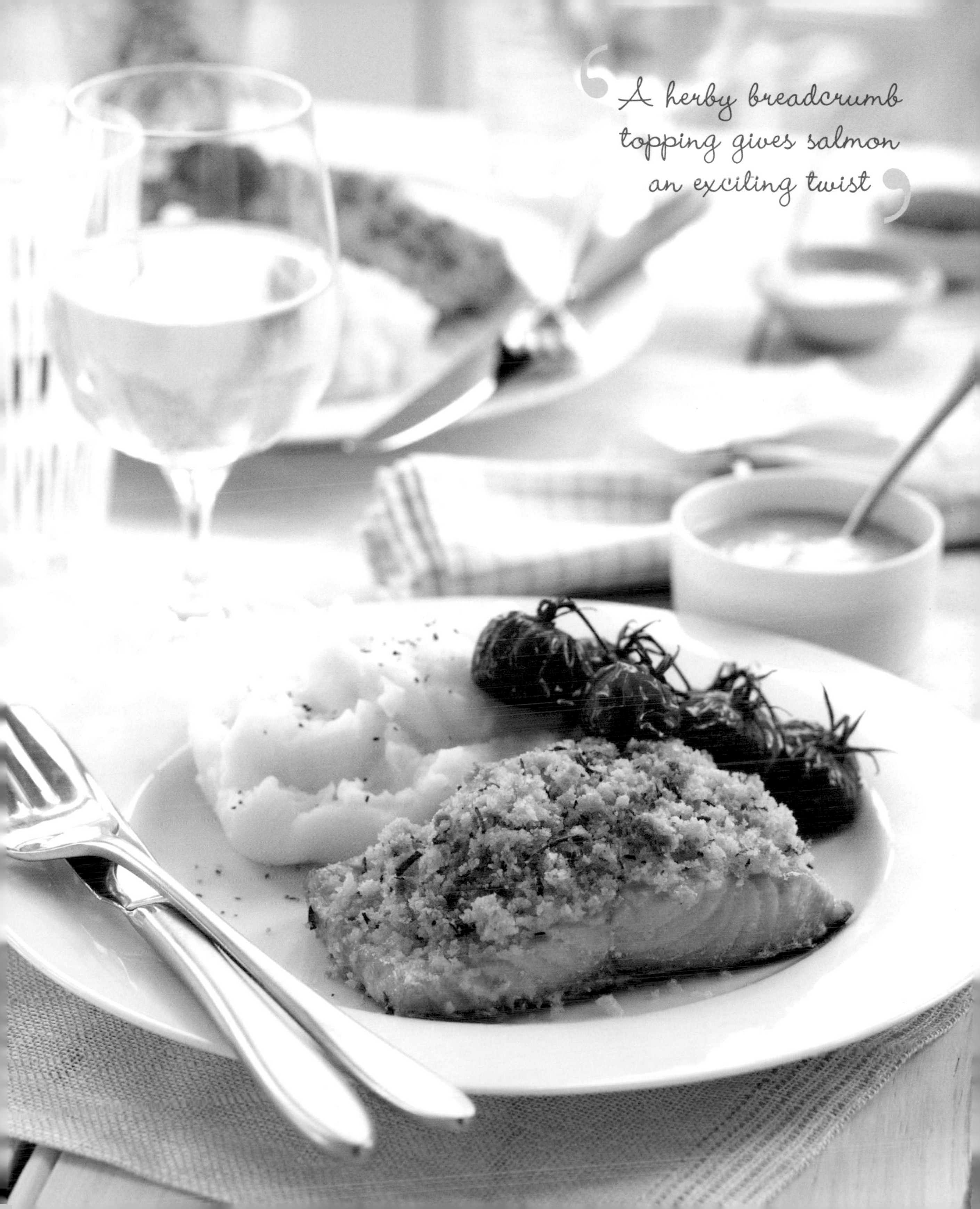

Serves 2
Prep time: 15 minutes
Cook time: 25 minutes

Zesty haddock parcels

The orange zest gives the haddock fillets a lovely citrus flavour in a recipe that's great cooked in the oven or on the barbecue

100g couscous
½ x red onion, peeled and thinly sliced
½ x 175g pack Sainsbury's baby corn and mange tout, the baby corn halved lengthways

2 x 100g haddock fillets, from the fish counter
zest of 1 orange

1   Preheat the oven to 200ºC, fan 180ºC, gas 6. Prepare the couscous following pack instructions.

2   Cut 2 x 36cm square pieces of foil and 2 x 36cm square pieces of baking parchment. Place the baking parchment on top of the foil.

3   Spoon the couscous into the centre of each piece of baking parchment. Top with the onion, baby corn and mange tout. Place the fish on top. Sprinkle the orange zest over the fish. Season with freshly ground black pepper, then fold up the foil/baking parchment to create a loose parcel (the ends should be tight so steam is created while cooking).

4   Place the parcels on a baking tray and cook in the oven for 25 minutes. To serve, simply unfold the packages and check the fish is fully cooked and piping hot before serving.

Per serving: 322 cals, 1.4g fat, 0.2g sat fat, 5.4g total sugars, 0.2g salt

Great for the barbecue...
This haddock dish is also great barbecued – make sure the grill is hot, then cook in the foil and baking parchment for 12–14 minutes, until cooked through

Unwrap the parcel and your senses are hit with a gorgeous citrus aroma

Serves 4
Prep time: 10 minutes
Cook time: 10 minutes

Oriental stir-fried prawns

Super quick and bursting with oriental flavours, this prawn and noodle dish is fast food at its best and is ideal for a light summer meal

1 tablespoon sesame oil
1 clove garlic, peeled and finely chopped
150g Chinese leaf, shredded
1 red pepper, deseeded and sliced
1 x 175g pack Sainsbury's baby corn & mange tout

1 x 225g pack frozen Taste the Difference jumbo king prawns, defrosted
1 tablespoon fish sauce
1 x 410g pack Sainsbury's fresh free-range egg noodles
100g beansprouts
zest and juice of 1 lime

1 Heat the sesame oil in a wok or large frying pan over a medium-high heat. Add the garlic, Chinese leaf, red pepper, baby corn and mange tout and stir-fry for 3–4 minutes.

2 Add the prawns, fish sauce and noodles and cook for a further 2 minutes. Stir through the beansprouts, lime zest and lime juice just before serving.

Per serving: 292 cals, 6.9g fat, 1.1g sat fat, 5.2g total sugars, 1.6g salt

Time-saving tip...
To speed things up, you could use Sainsbury's mixed pepper stir-fry instead of the individual vegetables listed here

This noodle dish is full of vitality and takes only minutes to prepare

Serves 4
Prep time: 25 minutes
Cook time: 50 minutes

Fish & chips
with tartare sauce & mushy peas

A tasty take on traditional fish and chips, without the deep-frying, served with a delicious homemade tartare sauce and mushy peas

750g Maris Piper potatoes, cut into wedges
2 tablespoons olive oil
4 x 200g cod loins, from the fish counter
50g plain flour
1 large egg, lightly beaten
1-2 tablespoons semi-skimmed milk
1 x 100g pack Sainsbury's Signature breadcrumbs

FOR THE MUSHY PEAS

500g frozen peas
6 mint leaves, chopped
4 tablespoons half-fat crème fraîche

FOR THE TARTARE SAUCE

4 tablespoons Sainsbury's light mayonnaise
2 baby gherkins, finely diced
1 teaspoon capers, finely chopped
2 tablespoons fresh flat-leaf parsley, chopped
juice of 1/2 x lemon

1 Preheat the oven to 200°C, fan 180°C, gas 6.

2 Place the potato wedges on a baking tray and drizzle over 1 tablespoon oil. Toss the potatoes to coat, then season well with salt and freshly ground black pepper. Bake for 45–50 minutes, turning halfway.

3 Meanwhile, season the fish with salt and freshly ground black pepper and dip in the flour. Mix the egg and milk together in a shallow dish. Dip the fish in the egg mixture and then in the breadcrumbs to coat.

4 Place the fish on a non-stick baking tray and drizzle with the remaining 1 tablespoon oil. When the potatoes have been cooking for 30 minutes, add the fish to the oven and bake for 15–20 minutes, until crisp and golden.

5 Meanwhile, place the peas in a pan of boiling water and simmer for 2–3 minutes over a medium-high heat. Drain, reserving 2 tablespoons cooking water. Stir the mint leaves, crème fraîche and reserved cooking water into the peas, then crush with a fork and season to taste.

6 Mix together all the ingredients for the tartare sauce. Serve with the fish, potato wedges and mushy peas.

Per serving: 542 cals, 19.3g fat, 4.2g sat fat, 6.9g total sugars, 1.1g salt

'Fish, chips and mushy peas – a British classic you can make at home'

Serves 4
Prep time: 10 minutes
Cook time: 35 minutes

Coconut fish curry

Coconut milk gives this curry a deliciously creamy flavour, and the almonds contrast well with the delicate texture of the fish

1 tablespoon sunflower oil
2 onions, peeled and sliced
2 red peppers, deseeded and diced
2 red chillies, deseeded and thinly sliced
1 tablespoon mild curry powder
1 x 400ml tin light coconut milk
100ml fish stock, made with 1/4 stock cube

450g trimmed monkfish or cod loin, from the fish counter, cut into large cubes
4 tablespoons toasted flaked almonds
1/2 x 28g pack Sainsbury's fresh coriander
steamed basmati rice, to serve
1 lime, cut into wedges

1 Heat the oil in a large, lidded pan and gently fry the onions for 10 minutes, until softened. Add the peppers, chillies and curry powder, and cook for another 2-3 minutes.

2 Pour in the coconut milk and fish stock. Simmer, uncovered, over a medium heat for 10 minutes.

3 Place the fish on top of the curry sauce, then cover the pan. Gently poach the fish for 8-10 minutes, until cooked through. Sprinkle over the almonds and coriander.

4 Serve the curry in bowls with steamed basmati rice and lime wedges to squeeze over.

Per serving: 549 cals, 19.7g fat, 10.4g sat fat, 11.7g total sugars, 0.1g salt

Serves 2 as starter
Prep time: 5 minutes
Cook time: 8 minutes

Pan-fried lime & chilli scallops

Sweet and succulent scallops are gorgeous pan-fried with oriental flavours. They're great as a starter, or serve them with new potatoes as a main

15g butter
200g frozen scallops
1 clove garlic, peeled and crushed
1 red chilli, deseeded and finely chopped
zest and juice of ½ x lime

2 tablespoons fresh coriander, chopped
40g watercress, spinach & rocket salad, to serve
lime wedges, to serve

1 Melt the butter in a frying pan over a medium-high heat. Add the frozen scallops and cook for 5 minutes, turning halfway, until hot and golden.

2 Add the garlic and chilli. Cook, stirring, for 1 minute, then remove from the heat.

3 Toss the lime zest, lime juice and coriander through the scallops. Serve with salad leaves and lime wedges, to squeeze over.

Per serving: 201 cals, 9.3g fat, 4.5g sat fat, 0.8g total sugars, 0.9g salt

Did you know...?
Sainsbury's frozen scallops are sourced from a sustainable fishery certified to the Marine Stewardship Council's standards

Serves 2
Prep time: 10 minutes
Cook time: 30 minutes

Roast monkfish

with cherry tomatoes & red onion

Monkfish is a firm-textured, meaty white fish which is great baked.
Here it works well with roasted vegetables and a sprinkling of parsley

4 cloves garlic, peeled and crushed

2 red onions, peeled and cut into 2cm wedges

2 tablespoons olive oil

1 x 225g pack Sainsbury's cherry tomatoes on the vine

2 fresh monkfish tails (or any other firm-fleshed white fish, such as cod loin), from the fish counter

2 tablespoons fresh flat-leaf parsley, chopped

1 lemon, cut into wedges, to garnish

1 Preheat the oven to 180°C, fan 160°C, gas 4.

2 Toss together the garlic, red onion wedges and 1 tablespoon oil. Place in a roasting tin and lay the vine tomatoes on top.

3 Lay the fish over the vegetables and drizzle with the remaining 1 tablespoon oil. Season with sea salt and freshly ground black pepper.

4 Bake for 30 minutes, or until the fish is cooked through. Serve scattered with fresh parsley and garnished with lemon wedges.

Per serving: 229 cals, 12g fat, 1.8g sat fat, 10.7g total sugars, trace salt

Did you know...?
All Sainsbury's monkfish is farmed off the southwest coast of England

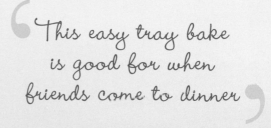

'This easy tray bake is good for when friends come to dinner'

Serves 4
Prep time: 15 minutes
Cook time: 10 minutes

Herby fish fingers

Made with pollock, a white fish similar in taste and texture to cod, these fish fingers will be a winner with the whole family

600g Sainsbury's pollock fillets, skin removed
juice of 1 lemon
50g plain flour
2 teaspoons cayenne pepper
2 eggs, lightly beaten

150g fresh breadcrumbs
15g fresh flat-leaf parsley, roughly chopped
2 tablespoons olive oil
tartare sauce, to serve
watercress, to serve

1 Preheat the oven to 150°C, fan 130°C, gas 2.

2 Slice the pollock fillets into 20 fingers. Pour the lemon juice into a bowl, add the fish and toss to coat.

3 Mix together the flour and cayenne pepper in a bowl. Pour the beaten egg into another bowl, and combine the fresh breadcrumbs and parsley in a third bowl. Roll each piece of fish first in the flour, then in the egg, then in the herby breadcrumbs. Place the fish on a plate and set aside.

4 Heat the oil in a frying pan over a medium heat and shallow-fry the fish fingers in batches for 1-2 minutes on each side. Keep the cooked fish fingers warm in the oven while cooking the rest. Serve with some tartare sauce and a few sprigs of peppery watercress.

Per serving: 484 cals, 19.5g fat, 2.9g sat fat, 2.4g total sugars, 1.6g salt

Did you know...?
Pollock is a lesser-known member of the cod family and is low in fat. Sainsbury's is passionate about sustainable sourcing and pollock is a green choice as it's in plentiful supply off the British coast

"These herby fish fingers are a fun way to get the kids to enjoy fish"

Serves 4
Prep time: 10 minutes
Cook time: 15 minutes

Seared tuna
with salsa verde & new potatoes

This vibrant, herby Italian sauce is all that's needed to give extra flavour to lightly seared tuna steaks

750g new potatoes
4 x 150g tuna steaks
1 x 70g pack Sainsbury's wild rocket leaves, to serve
lemon wedges, to serve

FOR THE SALSA VERDE
1 teaspoon capers, finely chopped
4 anchovy fillets, finely chopped
2 cloves garlic, peeled and finely chopped

1 x 28g pack Sainsbury's fresh flat-leaf parsley, finely chopped
1 x 28g pack Sainsbury's fresh mint, finely chopped
1 x 28g pack Sainsbury's fresh basil, finely chopped
1 tablespoon red wine vinegar
3 tablespoons extra virgin olive oil
$\frac{1}{2}$ teaspoon Dijon mustard
1 teaspoon lemon juice

1 Place the potatoes in a pan of cold water and bring to the boil, then reduce the heat and cook for 12 minutes, until tender. Drain.

2 Meanwhile, make the salsa verde. Place the capers, anchovies, garlic, parsley, mint and basil in a bowl. Stir in the red wine vinegar, olive oil, mustard and lemon juice, and whisk to a sauce consistency.

3 Preheat a non-stick griddle pan over a medium-high heat. Add the tuna steaks and cook for 1–2 minutes on each side. Serve with the salsa verde drizzled over, and the potatoes, rocket and lemon wedges.

Per serving: 437 cals, 10.3g fat, 2g sat fat, 3g total sugars, 0.4g salt

Fair on fish
Sainsbury's has been rated no. 1 for tinned tuna by Greenpeace as a result of its responsible sourcing credentials and business values

'Meaty tuna steaks are fantastic served with this zingy herb sauce'

Serves 4
Prep time: 20 minutes,
plus marinating time
Cook time: 20 minutes

Soy & citrus salmon salad

The lime and soy sauce marinade gives this salmon a rich flavour, and the salad adds a freshness to the dish

4 salmon fillets
juice of 2 limes
2 tablespoons reduced-salt soy sauce
1 tablespoon sesame or vegetable oil
2 teaspoons caster sugar
1 clove garlic, peeled and crushed

1 cucumber
1 x 75g bag Sainsbury's watercress, chopped
1 x 28g pack Sainsbury's fresh coriander,
leaves picked
$\frac{1}{2}$ x small red onion, peeled and thinly sliced

1 Place the salmon in a glass, plastic or stainless-steel bowl (these won't react with the acid in the lime juice). Mix together the lime juice, soy sauce, oil and sugar. Stir until the sugar has dissolved, then pour half the mixture into a jug for dressing the salad later. Add the garlic to the remaining mixture and pour over the salmon. Place in the fridge, covered, to marinate for 20 minutes.

2 Preheat the oven to 180°C, fan 160°C, gas 4. Heat a non-stick frying pan over a medium heat. Reserving the marinade, cook the salmon for 2–3 minutes on each side. Transfer the fish to a non-stick, shallow roasting tray and drizzle with some of the marinade. Season with salt and freshly ground black pepper and roast in the oven for 10–15 minutes, adding the rest of the marinade halfway through.

3 Meanwhile, using a peeler, cut the cucumber into long, thin ribbons. Place in a bowl and toss together with the watercress, coriander and onion. Dress the salad and serve with the salmon.

Per serving: 160 cals, 7.8g fat, 1.3g sat fat, 5.5g total sugars, 1g salt

Fair on fish
All Sainsbury's fresh and smoked salmon is 100%
Scottish and reared on Freedom Food farms that
meet RSPCA standards for welfare

‘Marinating the salmon infuses the fish with a tangy flavour’

Serves 4
Prep time: 20 minutes
Cook time: 10 minutes

Griddled sea bass

with minty green salad

Griddling sea bass gives it a deliciously crispy skin, and it's great served on a bed of minty green vegetables

---

475g courgettes, cut into thick slices
2 tablespoons olive oil
400g frozen broad beans
½ x 28g pack Sainsbury's fresh mint, finely chopped

1 x 75g bag Sainsbury's watercress, chopped
4 medium boneless sea bass fillets (or cod or haddock fillets), skin on, from the fish counter

---

1 Heat a griddle pan over a high heat. In a bowl, mix the courgette slices with 1 tablespoon olive oil and season with salt and freshly ground black pepper. Cook on the griddle for 2 minutes on each side, then return to the bowl.

2 Place the broad beans in a pan of boiling water and boil for 1 minute, then drain and remove the tough outer skins to reveal the bright green inner beans. Place in the bowl with the courgettes, then stir in the mint and watercress.

3 Meanwhile, keeping the griddle pan on medium-high, heat the remaining 1 tablespoon olive oil. Place the sea bass in the pan, skin-side down, and cook for 4–5 minutes, until the skin is crispy. Turn the fish over and cook for 1 minute, until the flesh is cooked through.

4 Serve the sea bass on top of the courgette and bean salad, skin-side up.

Per serving: 263 cals, 9.8g fat, 2g sat fat, 3.5g total sugars, 0.2g salt

Serves 4
Prep time: 15 minutes
Cook time: 10 minutes

King prawn bake & linguine

Sainsbury's lemon & black pepper breadcrumbs give these garlicky king prawns an irresistibly crunchy coating

2 x 180g packs Sainsbury's raw king prawns
4 cloves garlic, peeled and sliced
2 tablespoons white wine
30g unsalted butter, softened

4 tablespoons Sainsbury's lemon & black pepper breadcrumbs
2 tablespoons fresh flat-leaf parsley, chopped
320g linguine
juice of 3 lemons and zest of 2

1 Preheat the oven to 200°C, fan 180°C, gas 6.

2 Place the prawns, garlic and wine in a small ovenproof dish. Dot with the butter and top with the breadcrumbs and parsley. Season with freshly ground black pepper. Bake in the oven for 8-10 minutes, or until the prawns are opaque.

3 Meanwhile, heat a large pan of water until boiling, then add the linguine and cook, following pack instructions, until al dente. Drain and stir through the lemon juice, lemon zest and some freshly ground black pepper. Divide between 4 plates and top with the prawn bake.

Per serving: 440 cals, 8.4g fat, 5.2g sat fat, 3.4g total sugars, 2.1g salt

Cook's tip
To give this dish even more flavour and boost your vegetable intake, stir through some baby spinach leaves when you add the lemon zest

‘ For a pasta dish out
of the ordinary, try this
garlicky king prawn bake ’

Serves 4
Prep time: 15 minutes,
plus chilling time
Cook time: 40 minutes

Salmon & red onion fishcakes
with dill & garlic mayonnaise

Taste the Difference lightly smoked salmon fillets add a delicate smoky flavour to these extra-special fishcakes

2 x 260g packs Taste the Difference lightly smoked salmon fillets
700g Taste the Difference Vivaldi white potatoes, peeled
½ x red onion, peeled and finely chopped
zest of 1 lemon
½ x 28g pack Sainsbury's fresh flat-leaf parsley, chopped

2 tablespoons plain flour
1 egg, beaten
150g fresh white breadcrumbs
400ml vegetable oil, for shallow frying
¼ x 25g pack Sainsbury's fresh dill, chopped
100g Taste the Difference garlic mayonnaise
salad leaves, to serve
lemon wedges, to serve

1 Preheat the oven to 200ºC, fan 180ºC, gas 6. Place the fish on a lightly greased baking tray. Bake for 10-12 minutes, or until just cooked through. Flake, remove any bones, then leave to cool slightly.

2 Meanwhile, place the potatoes in a large pan of cold water and bring to the boil. Cook for 10-15 minutes, until tender, then drain and mash. Cool slightly.

3 In a large bowl, mix together the mash, onion, lemon zest and parsley. Season well with salt and freshly ground black pepper. Stir in the salmon, without breaking it up too much. Shape the mixture into 8 rounds. Place on a baking tray lined with baking parchment and chill in the freezer for 10 minutes.

4 Tip the flour, egg and breadcrumbs into 3 separate bowls. Coat the fishcakes in flour, shaking off the excess. Dip in the egg, then the breadcrumbs, coating well.

5 Heat the oil in a deep pan. Fry the fishcakes in batches for 2-3 minutes, until golden. Remove with a slotted spoon and place on a baking tray. Bake in the oven for 10-15 minutes, until piping hot. Mix the dill into the garlic mayonnaise. Serve the fishcakes with the mayonnaise, salad leaves and lemon wedges.

Per serving: 835 cals, 44.3g fat, 6.3g sat fat, 4.4g total sugars, 3g salt

"Packed with chunks of salmon, these fishcakes are hard to beat"

Serves 2
Prep time: 15 minutes
Cook time: 15 minutes

Pan-fried sea bream

with pineapple salsa

Sea bream is a firm-fleshed, succulent white fish with a similar flavour to sea bass, and works well with this sweet and spicy pineapple salsa

2 x 300g whole fresh sea bream (gutted and descaled), from the fish counter
1 tablespoon olive oil
1 or 2 limes, halved, to garnish

FOR THE PINEAPPLE SALSA
1 red chilli, deseeded and finely diced
$1/2$ x red onion, peeled and diced
220g fresh pineapple, peeled and finely diced
2 tablespoons fresh coriander, finely chopped, plus extra to garnish
zest and juice of 1 lime

1 To make the salsa, combine the chilli, onion, pineapple, coriander, lime juice and lime zest in a bowl, then set aside.

2 Preheat the oven to 200°C, fan 180°C, gas 6.

3 Heat an ovenproof frying pan on the hob. Brush the fish with the oil, then place in the hot pan and fry for about 5 minutes on one side, until it starts to colour. Carefully turn the fish over, then place the frying pan in the oven to finish cooking – this will take about 10-15 minutes, depending on the size of your fish.

4 Meanwhile, heat a griddle pan over a medium-high heat. Place the lime halves, cut-side down, on the griddle and cook for 1 minute, until lightly golden. Serve the bream with the salsa, garnished with coriander, with the griddled lime halves on the side.

Per serving: 359 cals, 13.1g fat, 0.8g sat fat, 13.6g total sugars, 0.7g salt

'This refreshing pineapple salsa will awaken your taste buds'

barbecues

The classic burger   118

Grilled Caesar chicken skewers   120

Lamb patties & mint yogurt sauce   122

Moroccan chicken parcels   124

Posh hot dogs   126

Barbecued steak with aioli   128

Pork, sage & leek kebabs   130

Chilli, soy & ginger marinated beef kebabs   130

Herby turkey burgers   132

Grilled halloumi with radish, apple & sweetcorn relish   134

Lentil & oat veggie burgers   136

Buttered-up corn on the cob   138

Easy sweetcorn relish   138

Homemade tomato ketchup   140

Homemade barbecue sauce   140

The classic burger

Serves 4
Prep time: 15 minutes,
plus chilling time
Cook time: 15 minutes

These juicy, homemade burgers will be the star of the show at your summer barbecues

1 x 500g pack Sainsbury's extra lean beef mince
1 onion, peeled and finely chopped
2 cloves garlic, peeled and crushed
1 teaspoon English mustard
1 tablespoon olive oil, plus extra for greasing

ACCOMPANIMENTS
4 tablespoons light mayonnaise
4 teaspoons wholegrain mustard
1 x pack 4 Sainsbury's heat & serve ciabatta rolls, cut in half
50g rocket leaves
4 x 30g slices Brie
1 red onion, peeled and sliced into rounds

1   In a large bowl, mix together the beef mince, onion, garlic, English mustard and oil. Divide the mixture into 4 balls, then flatten into patties. Place on a plate, cover with clingfilm and leave in the fridge to firm up for at least 1 hour, or overnight if you have time.

2   Preheat the barbecue. Rub a little oil over the burgers and grill them over a medium heat for 6-7 minutes on each side, or until cooked through.

3   Meanwhile, mix together the mayonnaise and wholegrain mustard in a small bowl. Grill the ciabatta rolls on the cut sides, then spread the mayonnaise mixture over the 4 bottom pieces and top with rocket leaves.

4   Place the burgers on the rocket and top with the Brie, onion slices and ciabatta tops. Serve immediately. Great with homemade ketchup (see page 140).

Per serving: 562 cals, 24.8g fat, 10.4g sat fat, 7.1g total sugars, 1.9g salt

Not barbecue weather?
Heat a griddle pan to a medium heat, rub the burgers with a little oil and fry them for 6-7 minutes on each side, or until cooked through

'Easy to make, this really is the ultimate burger'

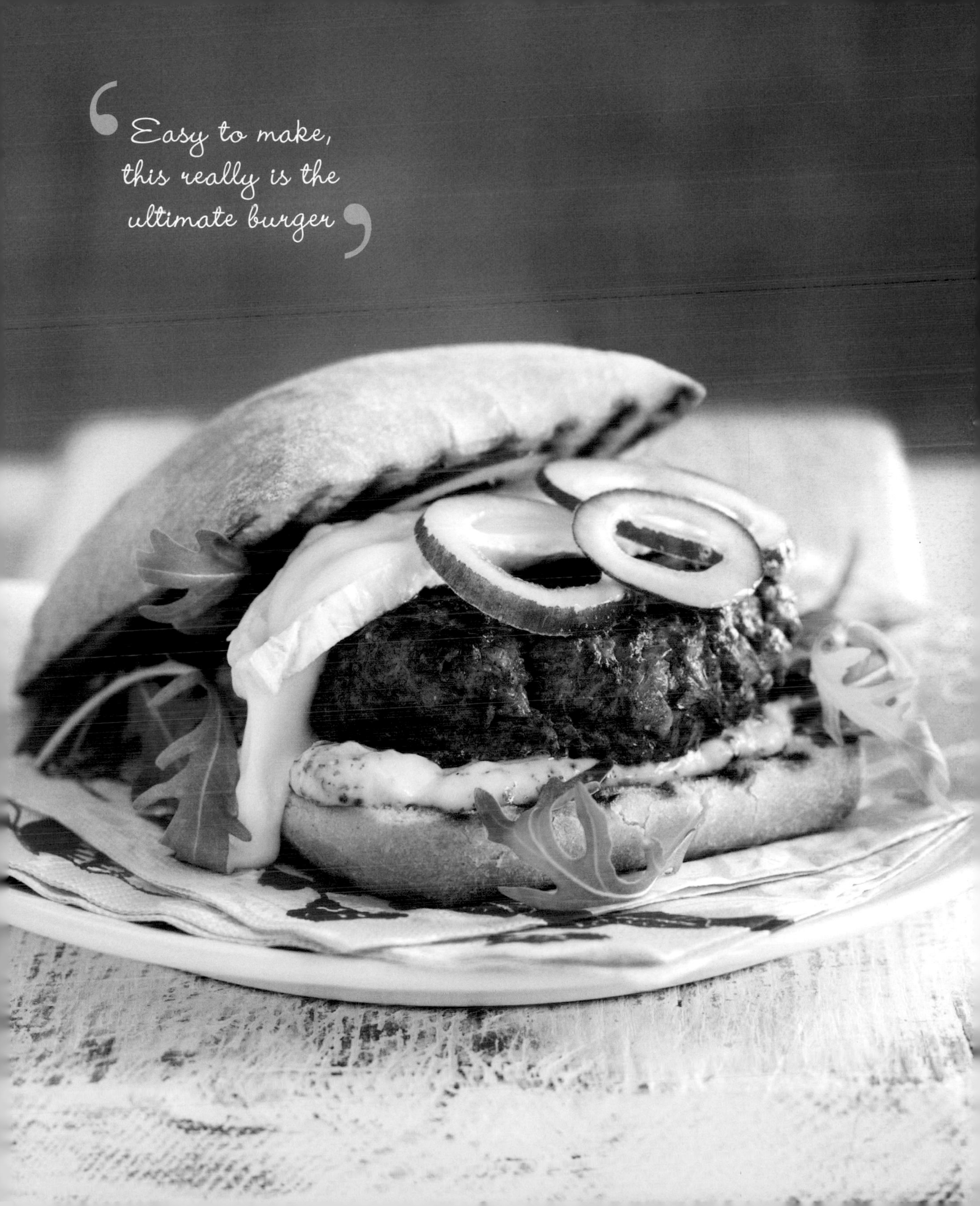

Serves 4
Prep time: 10 minutes,
plus marinating time
Cook time: 25 minutes

Grilled Caesar chicken skewers

An exciting twist on the classic Caesar salad, the chicken in this recipe is marinated in the Caesar dressing before being barbecued

500g skinless chicken fillets, cut into 2cm cubes
1 x 175ml bottle Sainsbury's fresh Caesar salad dressing
½ x 300g Taste the Difference garlic ciabatta, at room temperature

40g butter
100g smoked back bacon
1 x heart of romaine lettuce, cut into 4 wedges, and then cut in half
1 lemon, cut into wedges
You will also need 8 skewers

1 Place the chicken in a sealable plastic bag and pour in the whole bottle of Caesar dressing. Shake to mix together, then marinate in the fridge for at least 1 hour. If you're using wooden skewers, make sure you soak them in water for at least 30 minutes before cooking.

2 Preheat the barbecue.

3 Thread the chicken onto 8 skewers. Cook on a medium-hot grill for about 15 minutes, turning regularly, until cooked through. Set aside and keep warm.

4 Cut the ciabatta into 8 slices and butter each side. Toast on the barbecue for 1–2 minutes on each side, until golden. At the same time, grill the bacon for 5–10 minutes, until crispy, then cut into thin strips.

5 Place 2 chicken skewers on 2 slices of toasted ciabatta. Add 2 lettuce wedges to each plate, scatter over the bacon and serve with lemon wedges on the side.

Per serving: 641 cals, 40.3g fat, 11.5g sat fat, 2.4g total sugars, 1.5g salt

Did you know...?
All Sainsbury's fresh and frozen chicken is always
100% British

Serves 2
Prep time: 15 minutes,
plus chilling time
Cook time: 20 minutes

Lamb patties & mint yogurt sauce

These aromatic lamb patties make a change from burgers. They're easy to rustle up and are delicious served in pittas with a minty yogurt dip

½ x 500g pack Sainsbury's lamb mince
1 tablespoon Sainsbury's mint jelly
1 teaspoon cumin seeds
½ x beaten egg
50ml Sainsbury's be good to yourself Greek style natural yogurt

1 tablespoon fresh mint leaves, chopped
½ tablespoon olive oil
½ x 135g pack Sainsbury's cosmopolitan salad
60g cherry tomatoes, halved
2 pittas, split

1 Preheat the barbecue.

2 Combine the mince, mint jelly, cumin seeds and egg in a large bowl. Season with salt and freshly ground black pepper and shape into 4 small patties. Chill in the fridge for 10 minutes.

3 Meanwhile, pour the yogurt into a small bowl and mix in the mint. Season with salt and freshly ground black pepper and set aside.

4 Brush the patties with the olive oil, then cook over a medium-hot grill for 15-20 minutes, turning once, until cooked through.

5 Meanwhile, in a bowl, toss the salad with the cherry tomato halves. Toast the pittas.

6 Serve the patties in the toasted pittas with the minty yogurt sauce and salad.

Per serving: 706 cals, 31.4g fat, 13.6g sat fat, 10.7g total sugars, 1.6g salt

Freeze ahead tip
Double the lamb mixture, form into patties and freeze so you have them on hand for impromptu barbecues when the weather's good

Imagine the smell of
these juicy lamb patties
sizzling on the barbecue

Serves 4
Prep time: 15 minutes
Cook time: 30 minutes

Moroccan chicken parcels

A spiced-up couscous filling gives these tender chicken breasts an exciting Moroccan flavour

75g couscous
1 teaspoon ground cumin
1 tablespoon harissa paste
2 tablespoons fresh flat-leaf parsley, chopped
80g dried, ready to eat apricots, chopped
zest and juice of 1 lemon
4 skinless chicken breasts

1 teaspoon olive oil
4 teaspoons Sainsbury's Mediterranean style tomato & herb rub
1 x 270g pack Taste the Difference vittoria tomatoes
2 medium courgettes, cut into ribbons using a vegetable peeler

1 Preheat the barbecue to high.

2 Place the couscous in a bowl and pour over 160ml boiling water. Leave for 10 minutes, then stir through the cumin, harissa paste, parsley, apricots and lemon zest.

3 Make a deep slice horizontally in each chicken breast to create a pocket, making sure you don't cut all the way through. Pack a quarter of the couscous stuffing into each chicken breast pocket. Brush each chicken breast with oil and pat over the tomato & herb rub. Season with salt and freshly ground black pepper.

4 Cut 4 pieces of foil and place a chicken breast in the centre of each. Squeeze over a little lemon juice, then seal to form a parcel.

5 Place the foil parcels on the barbecue for 20 minutes, then remove and carefully undo. Add the tomatoes and courgettes, reseal and cook for a further 10 minutes, then serve.

Per serving: 380 cals, 4.7g fat, 1g sat fat, 11.3g total sugars, 0.6g salt

Not barbecue weather?
You could cook this chicken in an oven preheated to 220°C, fan 200°C, gas 7 for 25–30 minutes

‘Give chicken a Moroccan twist with fruity couscous’

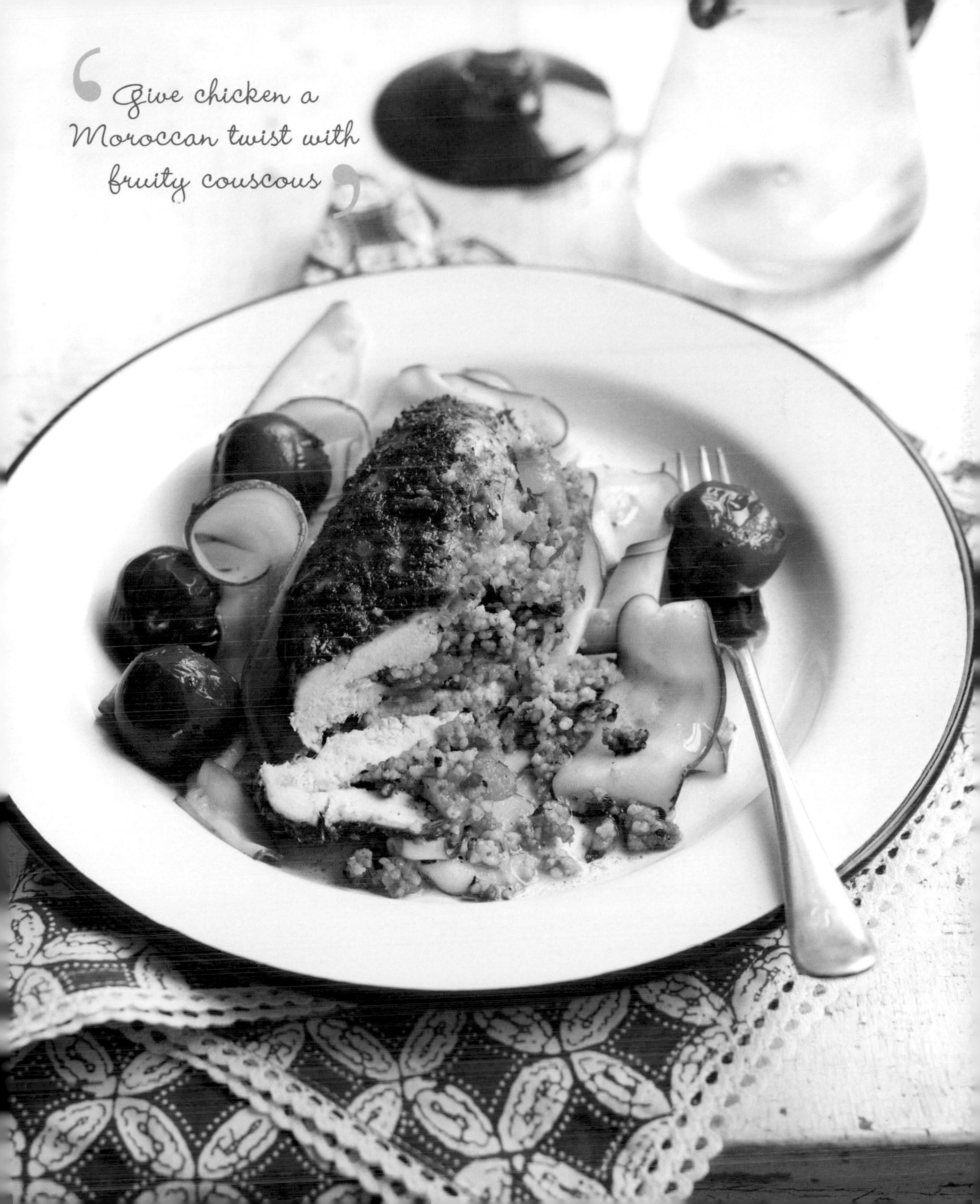

Serves 6
Prep time: 15 minutes
Cook time: 15 minutes

Posh hot dogs

Sausages are a much-loved barbecue essential – jazz them up with some homemade houmous

1 tablespoon honey
1 teaspoon ground cumin
1 x pack 6 Taste the Difference ultimate outdoor-bred pork sausages
6 Sainsbury's large multi-seeded deli sandwich rolls, sliced
1 x 80g bag Sainsbury's herb salad, to serve

FOR THE HOUMOUS
1 x 410g tin Sainsbury's chick peas, drained
2 tablespoons lemon juice
2 cloves garlic, peeled and crushed
1 teaspoon ground cumin
100g tahini
2 tablespoons olive oil
pinch of paprika

1 Preheat the barbecue to high.

2 Place all the ingredients for the houmous in a food processor along with 4 tablespoons water. Whizz until smooth.

3 Mix the honey and cumin together, then brush it on the sausages. Barbecue, turning every 5 minutes, for about 15 minutes, until golden.

4 Spread 2 tablespoons houmous onto each deli roll (store any leftover houmous in the fridge), and add a small handful of salad leaves. Pop in the sausages and serve.

Per serving: 507 cals, 23.7g fat, 5.8g sat fat, 6.5g total sugars, 1.6g salt

Gluten-free hot dogs
There are 4 varieties of gluten-free sausages in Sainsbury's Taste the Difference range – Fresh herb pork, Toulouse, Sicilian and Bramley apple & pork – perfect with Sainsbury's freefrom soft rolls if you're following a gluten-free diet

Serves 8
Prep time: 15 minutes
Cook time: 3 minutes

Barbecued steak with aioli

A juicy steak is sure to give the meat lovers at your barbecue something to smile about, especially when you serve it with this tangy aioli

8 x Taste the Difference traditional beef sirloin steaks (about 195g each)
2 x 100g packs Sainsbury's watercress, spinach & rocket salad
1 x 270g pack Taste the Difference vittoria tomatoes, halved

FOR THE AIOLI
2 egg yolks
2 cloves garlic, peeled and crushed
½ teaspoon Dijon mustard
pinch of sugar
150ml extra virgin olive oil
juice of 1 lemon

1 To make the aioli, place the egg yolks, garlic, mustard and sugar in a large bowl and whisk together using an electric hand mixer. While whisking, slowly drizzle in the oil until incorporated. Add the lemon juice and some freshly ground black pepper and mix again, adding a teaspoon or two of boiling water if the mixture is too thick. Chill in the fridge until you're ready to serve.

2 Preheat the barbecue to medium-high, then add the steaks and cook for 1½ minutes on each side, or until cooked to your liking. Serve with the aioli, salad and tomatoes.

Per serving: 447 cals, 27.7g fat, 5.6g sat fat, 1.4g total sugars, 0.5g salt

'Aioli adds extra lip-smacking flavour to a succulent grilled steak'

Marinated kebabs

Pork, sage & leek kebabs

400g pork tenderloin, cut into chunks
zest and juice of 1 lemon
1 tablespoon olive oil

½ x 20g pack Sainsbury's fresh sage
2 leeks, chopped into 1cm slices
You will also need 8 skewers

1 Preheat the barbecue to medium-high. If you are using wooden skewers, make sure you soak them in water for at least 30 minutes before cooking.

2 Place the pork in a bowl and add the lemon juice, lemon zest and olive oil. Leave to marinate for 30 minutes.

3 Thread the pork, sage leaves and leeks onto skewers and place on the barbecue. Cook for 4-5 minutes on each side.

SERVES 4 Prep time: 15 minutes, plus marinating time   Cook time: 10 minutes

Per serving: 229 cals, 9.1g fat, 1.8g sat fat, 1.6g total sugars, 0.3g salt

Chilli, soy & ginger marinated beef kebabs

450g sirloin steak, cut into thin strips
1 red chilli, deseeded and finely chopped
30g fresh ginger, peeled and grated
2 tablespoons light soy sauce

2 red peppers, deseeded and chopped into
medium-sized pieces
You will also need 8 skewers

1 Preheat the barbecue to medium-high. If you are using wooden skewers, make sure you soak them in water for at least 30 minutes before cooking.

2 Place the beef in a bowl with the chilli, ginger and soy sauce. Leave to marinate for 30 minutes.

3 Thread the beef and peppers alternately onto the skewers. Place on the barbecue and cook for 5 minutes, turning twice.

SERVES 4 Prep time: 15 minutes, plus marinating time   Cook time: 5 minutes

Per serving: 190 cals, 5.5g fat, 2.1g sat fat, 6.1g total sugars, 1.3g salt

'Marinating kebabs makes the meat so tender and flavoursome'

Serves 4
Prep time: 15 minutes,
plus chilling time
Cook time: 16 minutes

Herby turkey burgers

Turkey mince is a lean and tasty alternative to beef, and the herbs and pesto add fabulous flavour to these burgers

1 x 500g pack Sainsbury's be good to yourself turkey mince
1 small red onion, peeled and finely chopped
1 x 28g pack Sainsbury's fresh basil, leaves picked and finely chopped
1 x 28g pack Sainsbury's fresh flat-leaf parsley, leaves picked and finely chopped
1 tablespoon green pesto sauce
1 egg, beaten
½ teaspoon oil, for greasing

ACCOMPANIMENTS

1 x pack Sainsbury's 4 large multi-seeded deli sandwich rolls, sliced in half
40g light mayonnaise
4 curly leaf lettuce leaves
1 beef tomato, sliced
1 small avocado, peeled, stoned and sliced
1 small red onion, peeled and thinly sliced
4 tablespoons sweetcorn relish (see page 138)

1   Place the mince, onion, basil, parsley and pesto in a large bowl. Mix together, adding just enough egg to bind the mixture.

2   Divide the mixture into 4 balls and flatten into patties. Place on a plate and leave in the fridge to firm up for a couple of hours, or overnight if you have time.

3   Preheat the barbecue. Rub a little oil over the burgers and cook over a medium-high heat for 8 minutes on each side.

4   Meanwhile, toast the seeded rolls on the cut sides. Spread a little mayonnaise over the 4 bottom halves and top with lettuce and tomato.

5   Place the burgers on top, then add the avocado, onion and sweetcorn relish. Pop on the top halves of the deli rolls and serve.

Per serving: 554 cals, 21.3g fat, 4g sat fat, 9.8g total sugars, 1.5g salt

> These turkey burgers are great stacked with fresh accompaniments

Serves 4
Prep time: 10 minutes
Cook time: 5-8 minutes

Grilled halloumi

with spicy radish, apple & sweetcorn relish

Halloumi, a semi-hard, chewy cheese with a mild salty flavour, is fantastic grilled on the barbie as it retains its firm texture when cooked

1 Granny Smith apple, cored and finely diced
100g tinned or fresh sweetcorn (kernels only)
4 radishes, quartered and thinly sliced
1 teaspoon Sainsbury's easy chilli
(from a jar)
juice of 2 limes, plus 1 extra lime, cut into wedges, to serve

1 tablespoon olive oil, plus extra for brushing the cheese
1 x 250g pack Sainsbury's Cypriot halloumi cheese, cut into 8 equal slices
$\frac{1}{4}$ x 25g pack Sainsbury's fresh chives, finely chopped

1 Preheat the barbecue.

2 In a bowl, mix together the apple, sweetcorn, radishes, chilli, lime juice and olive oil. Season with freshly ground black pepper and set aside.

3 Brush each side of cheese with a little oil. Cook over a medium-hot grill until golden and softened.

4 Divide the relish between 4 plates. Top with the halloumi, sprinkle with chives and serve with a wedge of lime.

Per serving: 283 cals, 20.6g fat, 11.2g sat fat, 5.3g total sugars, 2.1g salt

Wine match
This halloumi salad would be great with a glass of chilled Verdicchio. Crisp, delicate and zesty, this Italian white wine has summery flavours of green apples, lemons and a touch of pear. Its zingy acidity is great for cleansing the palate after spicy food

'Grilled halloumi is a brilliant barbecue option for vegetarians'

barbecues

Lentil & oat veggie burgers

Serves 4 (makes 8)
Prep time: 15 minutes, plus chilling time
Cook time: 15 minutes

These mouthwatering burgers will keep the vegetarians happy at your barbecue, though you'll probably find everyone else wants one too!

200g Taste the Difference rolled porridge oats
1 tablespoon olive oil
1 onion, peeled and finely chopped
1 carrot, finely chopped
1 clove garlic, peeled and finely chopped

2 x 410g tins Sainsbury's green lentils, drained
zest of ½ x lemon
½ teaspoon dried crushed chilli
65g Sainsbury's West Country farmhouse mature Cheddar, finely grated
2 teaspoons tomato purée

1 Place 75g porridge oats in a food processor and whizz until fine.

2 Heat the oil in a pan and cook the onion and carrot for 5 minutes until soft, adding the garlic for the final minute. Pour into a bowl, then mix in the lentils, lemon zest, crushed chilli, cheese and tomato purée. Add the blended oats and 75g whole oats. Mix until combined.

3 Form into 8 burgers, then roll in the remaining 50g oats. Chill in the fridge for 30 minutes. Meanwhile, preheat the barbecue.

4 Place the burgers on the barbecue and cook for 5 minutes on each side, until golden. Great served with salad and a dollop of mayonnaise.

Per serving: 407 cals, 13.3g fat, 5.1g sat fat, 5.6g total sugars, 0.3g salt

Not barbecue weather?
These veggie burgers can also be cooked in a frying pan. Heat 1 tablespoon olive oil in a pan and fry the burgers for 2–3 minutes on each side

Serves 4
Prep time: 10 minutes
Cook time: 15 minutes

Buttered-up corn on the cob

Corn on the cob is a barbecue favourite. Give yours the wow factor with a simple herb or spice butter

4 corn on the cobs	50g butter, softened

1 Preheat the barbecue.

2 Grill the corn on the cobs for 10-15 minutes, turning regularly, until lightly chargrilled. Mix the butter with one of the following, then spread onto the barbecued corn:

- finely chopped fresh herbs

- deseeded and finely chopped chilli

- citrus zest

- finely chopped spring onion

- smoked paprika

Per serving: 223 cals, 12.5g fat, 6.9g sat fat, 2.5g total sugars, trace salt

Easy sweetcorn relish

Heat a large saucepan, add 2 teaspoons mustard seeds and cook for 2 minutes. Add the kernels from 2 sweetcorn cobs, 4 tablespoons cider vinegar, 1 teaspoon caster sugar, 2 deseeded and finely chopped red peppers, 1 peeled and finely chopped small red onion and 4 tablespoons water. Bring to the boil and simmer over a low heat for 8 minutes. Cool, then season and stir in 2 teaspoons chopped chives. Store in a sterilised jar in the fridge for up to 1 week.

MAKES 500G
Prep time: 10 minutes Cook time: 10 minutes

Per 100g: 56 cals, 1g fat, 0.1g sat fat, 4.4g total sugars, trace salt

Relishes

Homemade tomato ketchup

½ tablespoon olive oil
1 large onion, peeled and chopped
2 x 390g cartons Sainsbury's chopped
tomatoes

50g light muscovado sugar
75ml cider vinegar
1 teaspoon English mustard powder

1 Heat the olive oil in a pan, then add the onion and cook for 10 minutes, until soft.

2 Tip into a food processor. Add the remaining ingredients and whizz until smooth. Spoon into a pan and cook over a medium-low heat for 1 hour, stirring frequently. Cool and store in the fridge in a sterilised, airtight container for up to 2 weeks.

MAKES 300G   Prep time: 10 minutes   Cook time: 1 hour, 10 minutes   **V**

Per 100g: 45 cals, 0.8g fat, nil sat fat, 7.4g total sugars, trace salt

Homemade barbecue sauce

20g butter
1 large onion, peeled and very finely chopped
300g Sainsbury's tomato ketchup
75ml orange juice

2 tablespoons maple syrup
2 tablespoons dark muscovado sugar
2 tablespoons Worcestershire sauce

1 Melt the butter in a pan, then add the onion and cook until soft.

2 Add the remaining ingredients and cook over a medium-low heat for 45 minutes, stirring frequently, until the sauce has reduced and thickened. Cool and store in the fridge in a sterilised, airtight container for up to 2 weeks.

MAKES 350G   Prep time: 10 minutes   Cook time: 50 minutes

Per 100g: 119 cals, 2.7g fat, 2g sat fat, 19.2g total sugars, 0.7g salt

picnics

Courgette, pea & parmesan tart   144

Little pork & apricot parcels   146

Crispy fried chicken   148

Sweet soy chicken drumsticks   148

Vegetarian Scotch egg   150

Chorizo, manchego & pepper stratas   152

Herby sausage rolls   152

Courgette & cheese frittata   154

Creamy pea & feta pasta salad   156

New potato, soya bean & mint salad   156

Butternut squash, bacon & rice salad   158

Noodle salad with stir-fried vegetables   160

Chocky rocky road   162

Fruity bars   162

Courgette, pea & parmesan tart

Serves 8 (or 6 as a main course)
Prep time: 15 minutes, plus chilling time
Cook time: 20 minutes

Ideal for picnics, this tart also works well as a starter or vegetarian main course

1 x 500g pack Sainsbury's puff pastry, removed from fridge 1 hour before use
1 medium egg, beaten
200g soft white cheese
juice of 1 small lemon

4 tablespoons freshly grated parmesan
60g frozen peas
2-3 courgettes, peeled into ribbons
6 spring onions, roughly sliced at an angle
1 tablespoon extra virgin olive oil

1 Preheat the oven to 200°C, fan 180°C, gas 6.

2 Roll out the pastry into a large rectangle, ½ cm thick. Cut to a 30 x 21cm rectangle and use a knife to mark out a border about 2½ cm inside the edge. Using a sharp knife, mark a lattice pattern on the borders, then brush with the egg. Place on a baking tray and refrigerate while you prepare the other ingredients.

3 In a bowl, lightly mix together the soft cheese, lemon juice and 2 tablespoons parmesan. Season with a little salt and plenty of freshly ground black pepper, then spread over the pastry. Press the peas into the tart and pile on the courgette ribbons (they shrink down during cooking). Scatter over the spring onions and remaining 2 tablespoons parmesan.

4 Drizzle with the oil and bake for 20 minutes, or until the pastry is golden and the courgette looks wrinkly and soft.

Per serving: 444 cals, 33g fat, 14.3g sat fat, 2.9g total sugars, 1.1g salt

Makes 8
Prep time: 20 minutes
Cook time: 30 minutes

Little pork & apricot parcels

These little parcels are best served warm, so prepare them the night before and keep them in the fridge, ready to bake before your picnic

1 teaspoon olive oil

½ x onion, peeled and chopped

½ x carrot (about 40g), grated

½ x 500g pack Sainsbury's be good to yourself British pork mince

5 dried apricots, finely chopped

1 teaspoon fresh rosemary, leaves chopped

8 sheets fresh ready-rolled filo pastry

50g butter, melted

1 teaspoon sesame seeds

1 teaspoon poppy seeds

1   Heat the oil in a small pan. Add the onion and cook, stirring, until it has softened and is beginning to brown - this will take about 5 minutes.

2   Stir in the carrot and cook for another minute. Transfer to a bowl, then stir in the pork mince, apricots and rosemary. Mix well using your hands, then divide into 8 portions.

3   Preheat the oven to 180°C, fan 160°C, gas 4. Lay out 1 sheet of filo and brush half lengthways with a little butter. Fold the pastry in half lengthways to make one long strip. Place 1 portion of the pork mixture at the top. Fold the pastry and filling over at right angles to make a triangle, and continue folding to form a neat triangular parcel. Seal with a little melted butter. Repeat with the remaining pastry and pork mixture to make 8 parcels.

4   Place on a baking tray, brush with the remaining butter and sprinkle with sesame and poppy seeds. Bake for 20-25 minutes, until the parcels are golden and crisp. They are best served warm, so once cooked, wrap in foil and transport to your picnic.

Per parcel: 193 cals, 9.4g fat, 4.2g sat fat, 3.8g total sugars, 0.2g salt

‘These savoury pastries
are stuffed with herby
pork and apricots’

Serves 8
Prep time: 10 minutes
Cook time: 25 minutes

Crispy fried chicken

With their irresistible crunchy topping, these pieces of crispy chicken won't hang around for long

125g cornflour
2 teaspoons salt
1 tablespoon freshly ground black pepper
¼ tablespoon bicarbonate of soda
1 tablespoon paprika

100g cornflakes, crushed finely
1 egg, beaten
8 chicken pieces (thighs and legs), skin on
vegetable oil, for deep frying

1 Preheat the oven to 200°C, fan 180°C, gas 6.

2 Place the cornflour, salt, pepper, bicarbonate of soda, paprika and cornflakes in a resealable plastic bag. Seal and shake to mix.

3 Pour the egg into a bowl. Dip in the chicken pieces, then place in the bag one at a time and shake to coat.

4 In a large, deep pan, heat 2 inches of oil. Fry the chicken in the hot oil (don't overcrowd - cook in batches if necessary) for about 5 minutes, until golden. Remove from the oil, place on a baking tray and bake in the oven for 15-20 minutes, until cooked through.

Per serving: 551 cals, 30.4g fat, 6.3g sat fat, 1.1g total sugars, 1.7g salt

Sweet soy chicken drumsticks

In a bowl, mix together 75ml light soy sauce, 1 tablespoon vegetable oil, 3 tablespoons runny honey and 1 clove garlic, peeled and crushed. Place 8 Sainsbury's chicken drumsticks in a large bowl, pour over the marinade and leave in the fridge for 1 hour, or overnight if you have time. Arrange the drumsticks in a roasting tin and cook in a preheated oven at 200°C, fan 180°C, gas 6 for 15-20 minutes.

SERVES 8
Prep time: 5 minutes, plus marinating time Cook time: 20 minutes

Per serving: 211 cals, 9.2g fat, 2.3g sat fat, 5.8g total sugars, 1.5g salt

Makes 4
Prep time: 25 minutes
Cook time: 12 minutes

Vegetarian Scotch egg

With a fabulous cumin-spiced coating made from chick peas and kidney beans, these veggie Scotch eggs will be a hit with both vegetarians and meat eaters

6 medium eggs
1 tablespoon olive oil
1 onion, peeled and finely chopped
1 carrot, grated
1 clove garlic, peeled and finely chopped
1 x 410g tin Sainsbury's chick peas, drained
1 x 410g tin Sainsbury's kidney beans, drained
zest and juice of $\frac{1}{2}$ x lemon

$\frac{1}{4}$ teaspoon ground cumin
1 tablespoon fresh flat-leaf parsley, finely chopped
40g plain flour
100g fresh breadcrumbs
1 litre vegetable oil, for deep frying
$\frac{1}{2}$ x slice of bread, for checking the temperature of the oil

1 Place 4 eggs in a pan of boiling water and cook for 6 minutes. Drain and run under cold water, then peel off the shells.

2 Meanwhile, heat the olive oil in another pan, then add the onion and carrot and cook for 4 minutes, until softened but not coloured. Add the garlic and cook for 1 minute, then tip into a bowl.

3 Place the chick peas, kidney beans, lemon zest, lemon juice and cumin in a food processor and blend until puréed. Spoon into the bowl with the carrot and onion, then add the parsley and stir until combined.

4 Beat together the remaining 2 eggs. Tip the flour, beaten egg and breadcrumbs into 3 separate bowls. Roll the boiled eggs in the flour, then mould $\frac{1}{4}$ of the chick pea mixture onto each egg. Roll again in flour, then dip in the beaten egg and roll in the breadcrumbs.

5 Pour the vegetable oil into a large, high-sided pan and place over a medium heat. The oil is hot enough when $\frac{1}{2}$ x slice of bread takes 30 seconds to turn golden. Gently place the eggs into the oil and fry for 30–60 seconds on each side (the oil should only come halfway up the eggs). Drain on kitchen paper. Serve warm, or cold at your picnic.

Per serving: 432 cals, 19.2g fat, 3g sat fat, 6g total sugars, 0.5g salt

Chorizo, manchego & pepper stratas

Makes 12
Prep time: 20 minutes, plus standing and cooling time
Cook time: 35 minutes

These fluffy stratas are given a Spanish twist with chorizo and manchego

6 medium eggs
350ml semi-skimmed milk
100ml half-fat crème fraîche
½ x 150g pack Sainsbury's diced chorizo
100g manchego, grated

100g Sainsbury's roast pepper antipasto, drained and chopped
2 tablespoons chopped fresh chives
150g baguette, torn into 2cm chunks

1 Cut 12 x 14cm diameter circles out of baking parchment, then mould into the holes of a 12-hole muffin tin.

2 In a large bowl, beat the eggs with the milk and crème fraîche. Stir through the chorizo, manchego, peppers and chives.

3 Place the baguette in the parchment cases. Pour over the egg mixture and leave to soak for 30 minutes. Preheat the oven to 180°C, fan 160°C, gas 4.

4 Cook the stratas for 30–35 minutes, until set and golden. Cool for 15 minutes before serving.

Per strata: 161 cals, 9.9g fat, 5.1g sat fat, 2g total sugars, 0.6g salt

Herby sausage rolls

Preheat the oven to 200°C, fan 180°C, gas 6. In a bowl, mix 2 grated carrots, 1 finely chopped onion, 70g Sainsbury's breadcrumbs, 500g pork sausagemeat and ½ x 15g pack thyme leaves. Thinly roll out 500g puff pastry and cut into 4 long pieces. Spread each with sausagemeat, leaving a 1cm edge, then tightly roll up. Brush with beaten egg and sprinkle with 1 tablespoon poppy seeds. Cut each roll into 6 pieces. Bake on a greased baking tray for 15–20 minutes.

Makes 24 Prep time: 20 minutes Cook time: 20 minutes

45 mins

Each: 162 cals, 10.8g fat, 3.9g sat fat, 1.3g total sugars, 0.5g salt

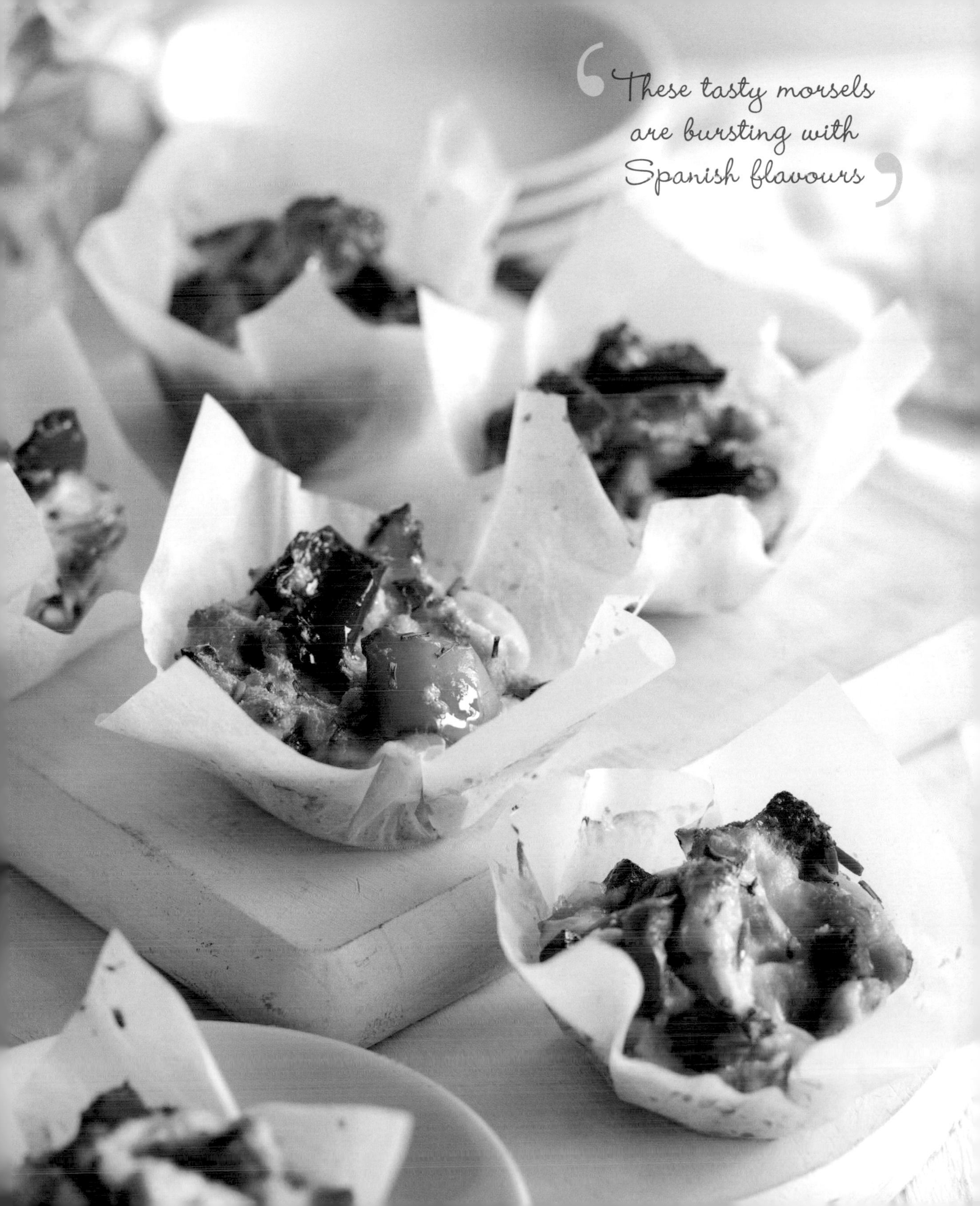

"These tasty morsels are bursting with Spanish flavours"

Serves 8
Prep time: 15 minutes
Cook time: 40 minutes

Courgette & cheese frittata

These mini frittata bites are perfect for picnics, and they're also great served warm with salad for a light summer lunch

500g Jersey Royals or small new potatoes
1 tablespoon fresh mint, chopped, plus
1 sprig for cooking the potatoes
25g butter
450g courgettes (about 2 large), coarsely grated

150g frozen peas
6 large eggs
75g mature Cheddar, grated
1 rounded tablespoon grated parmesan

1 Cook the potatoes with the sprig of mint in a pan of boiling water for 10-15 minutes, until tender. Drain. When cool enough to handle, cut into thick slices.

2 Meanwhile, heat the butter in a large frying pan. When it's bubbling, add the courgettes and cook for 3 minutes, stirring all the time. Add the frozen peas and cook for another 2 minutes. Remove the pan from the heat and stir in the chopped mint and sliced potatoes.

3 Line the base of a 27 x 16.5cm (4cm deep) roasting tray with baking parchment, then tip in the mixture.

4 Preheat the oven to 180°C, fan 160°C, gas 4. Beat the eggs in a bowl and stir in the Cheddar and a little freshly ground black pepper. Pour over the courgettes and potatoes. Sprinkle over the parmesan and bake for 20-25 minutes, until the egg has set.

5 Allow to cool for 10 minutes. Use a palette knife to go round the edges, then remove from the tin and discard the baking parchment. Cut into squares.

Per serving: 216 cals, 12.4g fat, 6.1g sat fat, 2.3g total sugars, 0.4g salt

Did you know...?
Sainsbury's was the first major supermarket to source all its whole eggs from cage-free hens, improving the lives of 800,000 birds

Scrummy bite-sized nibbles,
full of summer ingredients

Serves 6
Prep time: 15 minutes
Cook time: 15 minutes

Creamy pea & feta pasta salad

This appetising pasta salad is full of wonderful seasonal flavours

1 x 500g pack Sainsbury's conchiglie pasta
300g frozen petits pois
½ x 28g pack Sainsbury's fresh mint, leaves picked
juice of 1 lemon

100ml half-fat crème fraîche
1 x 50g pack Sainsbury's pea shoots
½ x 200g pack Sainsbury's Greek feta, broken into small pieces
50g Sainsbury's toasted seed mix

1 Place the pasta in a pan of boiling salted water. Cook for 10–12 minutes, then drain and allow to cool.

2 Meanwhile, cook the petits pois in a pan of boiling salted water for 2–3 minutes, then drain. Place in a food processor with the mint leaves and lemon juice, and blend until puréed. Tip into a medium-sized bowl and fold through the crème fraîche. Season to taste with freshly ground black pepper.

3 Toss the pasta with the pea purée, pea shoots, feta and seeds. Season with freshly ground black pepper, then transfer to your picnic container.

Per serving: 463 cals, 11.8g fat, 5.7g sat fat, 4.9g total sugars, 0.6g salt

New potato, soya bean & mint salad

Bring a large pan of water to the boil and cook 1kg new potatoes, halved, for around 20 minutes, until tender. Add 240g frozen soya beans for the last couple of minutes of cooking. (Alternatively, you could add broad beans for the last 4 minutes.) Drain well, then tip into a bowl and toss with 4 tablespoons half-fat crème fraîche and 1 x 28g pack Sainsbury's fresh mint, leaves shredded.

Serves 6 Prep time: 5 minutes Cook time: 20 minutes

Per serving: 295 cals, 9.3g fat, 2.2g sat fat, 4.7g total sugars, trace salt

Serves 6
Prep time: 20 minutes
Cook time: 35 minutes

Butternut squash, bacon & rice salad

A rice salad is a picnic essential, and sweet, roasted butternut squash, crispy bacon and crunchy cucumber make this one extra special

800g butternut squash, peeled and chopped into $^2/_3$ cm cubes
1 small red chilli, deseeded and finely chopped
1$^1/_2$ tablespoons olive oil
200g basmati rice
1 x 250g pack Sainsbury's smoked bacon lardons
$^1/_2$ x cucumber, halved horizontally and sliced into $^1/_2$ cm diagonal slices

2 tablespoons fresh flat-leaf parsley, roughly chopped

FOR THE DRESSING
1 tablespoon balsamic vinegar
3 tablespoons olive oil
$^1/_2$ tablespoon white wine vinegar
1 teaspoon sugar
1 teaspoon wholegrain mustard

1 Preheat the oven to 200°C, fan 180°C, gas 6.

2 Place the butternut squash and chilli on a baking tray. Drizzle with 1 tablespoon olive oil, season with salt and freshly ground black pepper and stir until combined. Roast for 25–30 minutes, until tender and turning golden. Remove from the oven and allow to cool slightly.

3 Meanwhile, cook the rice following pack instructions. Drain and cool in a sieve under cold running water, then set aside.

4 In a small frying pan, heat $^1/_2$ tablespoon olive oil and fry the bacon lardons until crispy. Drain on kitchen paper and set aside.

5 In a small bowl, mix all the dressing ingredients together. Place the butternut squash, rice, bacon and cucumber in a large bowl. Pour over the dressing and stir to combine. Sprinkle over the parsley and serve, or transfer to a picnic container.

Per serving: 350 cals, 16.8g fat, 5.2g sat fat, 7.8g total sugars, 1.4g salt

Serves 4
Prep time: 10 minutes
Cook time: 5 minutes

Noodle salad with stir-fried vegetables

This quick and easy salad is full of oriental flavours and makes a nice change for a picnic. It's also great served warm for a summer meal

1 tablespoon sesame oil

1 x 700g pack Sainsbury's basics vegetable stir-fry

1 red pepper, deseeded and sliced into strips

100g closed cup mushrooms, quartered

1 x 410g pack Sainsbury's fresh egg noodles

1 x 175ml pouch Sainsbury's Chinese stir-fry sauce

2 spring onions, sliced diagonally

1 Heat a wok over a high heat and add the sesame oil. Stir in the vegetable stir-fry, pepper and mushrooms and stir-fry for 3 minutes. Tip in the noodles and the Chinese sauce, stir together and cook for another 2 minutes.

2 Allow to cool, then transfer to a plastic container. Garnish with the spring onions and take on your picnic.

Per serving: 325 cals, 10.1g fat, 1g sat fat, 13g total sugars, 1.9g salt

Make it meaty

For a more substantial noodle salad, stir-fry strips of chicken or pork for 5 minutes, or until cooked through, before adding the vegetable stir-fry

Makes 20
Prep time: 10 minutes,
plus chilling time
Cook time: 10 minutes

Chocky rocky road

Packed with tasty chunks of biscuit and chewy marshmallow, these crunchy bars are the perfect sweet treat for a picnic

125g unsalted butter	200g digestive biscuits
300g dark chocolate, broken	100g Sainsbury's marshmallows, quartered
3 tablespoons golden syrup	1 teaspoon icing sugar, for dusting

1 Line a 23cm square cake tin with baking parchment.

2 Place the butter, chocolate and golden syrup in a saucepan. Gently heat until melted, then set aside to cool slightly.

3 Crush the biscuits, leaving some bits chunky, and fold into the chocolate mixture, along with the marshmallows. Spoon the mixture into the tin and smooth slightly with the back of a spoon. Place in the fridge for 4 hours to set. To serve, dust with the icing sugar and cut into 20 fingers.

Per serving: 196 cals, 11.9g fat, 7.4g sat fat, 14.1g total sugars, 0.2g salt

Fruity bars

Preheat the oven to 180°C, fan 160°C, gas 4. In a large pan over a medium heat, melt 100g unsalted butter, 75g golden syrup and 100g light brown sugar. Remove from the heat and stir in 200g porridge oats, 100g dried apricots, sliced, 50g seedless raisins and 2 tablespoons each poppy seeds and pumpkin seeds. Press the mixture into a 20 x 30cm baking tray lined with baking parchment. Bake for 25–30 minutes, until just turning golden at the edges. Let cool for 10–15 minutes, then cut into 18 bars.

Makes 18 Prep time: 10 minutes Cook time: 35 minutes (V) (45 mins)

Per serving: 153 cals, 6.9g fat, 3.4g sat fat, 12.8g total sugars, trace salt

desserts

Ice cream snowballs 166

Super-simple vanilla ice cream 166

Summer berry jelly 168

Sunshine strawberries with clotted cream 168

Eton mess with brown sugar meringues 170

Peach & amaretti fool 172

Chocolate mousse cake 174

Ginger parfait 176

Summer puddings 178

Barbecued nectarines with mascarpone cream 178

Cocktail jellies 180

Thai coconut sorbet 182

Strawberry marble mousse 184

Fig & berry no-bake cheesecakes 186

Fruit & nut knickerbocker glory 188

Ice cream snowballs

These gorgeous desserts are the perfect cooling treat for a summer's day, and they're even easier to make if you use shop-bought ice cream

150g chopped hazelnuts	8 scoops vanilla ice cream (see recipe below)
100g desiccated coconut	8 scoops chocolate ice cream

1 Place the chopped nuts and desiccated coconut in 2 separate bowls.

2 Roll half the scoops of ice cream in the nuts and half in the coconut, then place in serving bowls.

Per serving: 435 cals, 37.7g fat, 18.8g sat fat, 14.6g total sugars, 0.1g salt

Serving suggestion
These snowballs are also lovely coated with your favourite candy sweets, crushed up

Super-simple vanilla ice cream
Place 200g condensed milk, 600ml double cream and 1 teaspoon vanilla extract in a large bowl and whisk with an electric hand mixer until quite stiff. Spoon into a freezer-proof container, cover and freeze overnight. For other tasty options, stir in the following before freezing:
• 4 tablespoons Irish cream liqueur and 100g Sainsbury's mini fudge chunks
• 200g crushed raspberries and the seeds of 1 vanilla pod

MAKES 1 LITRE Prep time: 15 minutes, plus freezing time Ⓥ

Per serving (125ml vanilla): 415 cals, 37.7g fat, 23g sat fat, 15.8g total sugars, trace salt

'Irresistible scoops of ice cream coated with chopped nuts and coconut'

Serves 8
Prep time: 10 minutes
Setting time: 4 hours

Summer berry jelly

This jelly is so easy to make, and it's a great way to enjoy seasonal berries

150g blueberries
170g raspberries
½ x 454g pack Sainsbury's strawberries, hulled and sliced

2 x 135g packs strawberry jelly, cut into chunks
400ml Sainsbury's be good to yourself white grape & peach juice drink

1 Line a 1.5-litre loaf tin by placing a large piece of clingfilm over it and pressing down into the corners. Tip in the berries, reserving a few to decorate.

2 Place the jelly in a heatproof bowl. Pour on 170ml boiling water and stir until the jelly dissolves. Add the juice drink and stir to combine. Pour over the berries in the loaf tin, then place in the fridge for about 4 hours to set.

3 Gently turn the tin upside down and ease the jelly onto a plate, removing the clingfilm. Serve garnished with the reserved berries.

Per serving: 142 cals, 0.1g fat, nil sat fat, 30.7g total sugars, nil salt

Did you know...?
In 2009, Sainsbury's replaced the plastic lids on strawberries with sealed film, saving 333 tonnes of plastic per year

Sunshine strawberries
with clotted cream

Hull and slice 1 x 454g pack Sainsbury's strawberries. Place in a bowl with 2 tablespoons caster sugar and 150ml Pimm's and leave, covered, in the fridge for at least 3 hours (or overnight if you have time). Divide the strawberries and the juice between 4 sundae glasses or bowls, and serve with dollops of Taste the Difference Cornish clotted cream.

SERVES 4 Prep time: 10 minutes, plus chilling time

Per serving: 150 cals, 6.6g fat, 3.4g sat fat, 20.2g total sugars, nil salt

'This glossy, jewel-
coloured jelly makes
a fabulous centrepiece'

Serves 4
Prep time: 30 minutes
Cook time: 2 hours,
plus cooling time

Eton mess
with brown sugar meringues

Brown sugar adds a real depth of flavour to the meringue in this classic English summer dessert

2 medium egg whites
60g caster sugar
60g light muscovado sugar
1 teaspoon vanilla extract
200ml whipping cream
1 tablespoon icing sugar
200ml half-fat crème fraîche
400g strawberries, hulled and chopped

FOR THE CHOCOLATE SAUCE
75g dark chocolate
15g unsalted butter
75ml semi-skimmed milk
1 tablespoon golden syrup or runny honey

1 Preheat the oven to 120°C, fan 100°C, gas ½. Line a baking tray with baking parchment.

2 Whisk the egg whites in a bowl, until stiff. While still whisking, add the caster and muscovado sugar a spoonful at a time. Add the vanilla extract and continue whisking until you have a smooth, shiny and thick mixture.

3 Place 8 spoonfuls of the mixture on the baking tray, at least 3cm apart. Place in the oven and cook for 1 hour, 45 minutes. Turn off the heat and leave the meringues to cool in the oven for at least 4 hours, or ideally overnight.

4 To make the chocolate sauce, place the chocolate, butter, milk and golden syrup or honey in a pan. Melt over a low heat and stir to combine. Allow to cool slightly.

5 Place the whipping cream and icing sugar in a bowl and whisk until firm peaks form, then fold in the crème fraîche. Crush the meringues into medium-sized pieces. Add half the meringue and strawberries to the cream mixture. Place alternate spoonfuls of the cream mixture and remaining strawberries and meringue in bowls or glasses. Pour over some chocolate sauce and serve.

Per serving: 592 cals, 36g fat, 23.1g sat fat, 56.3g total sugars, 0.1g salt

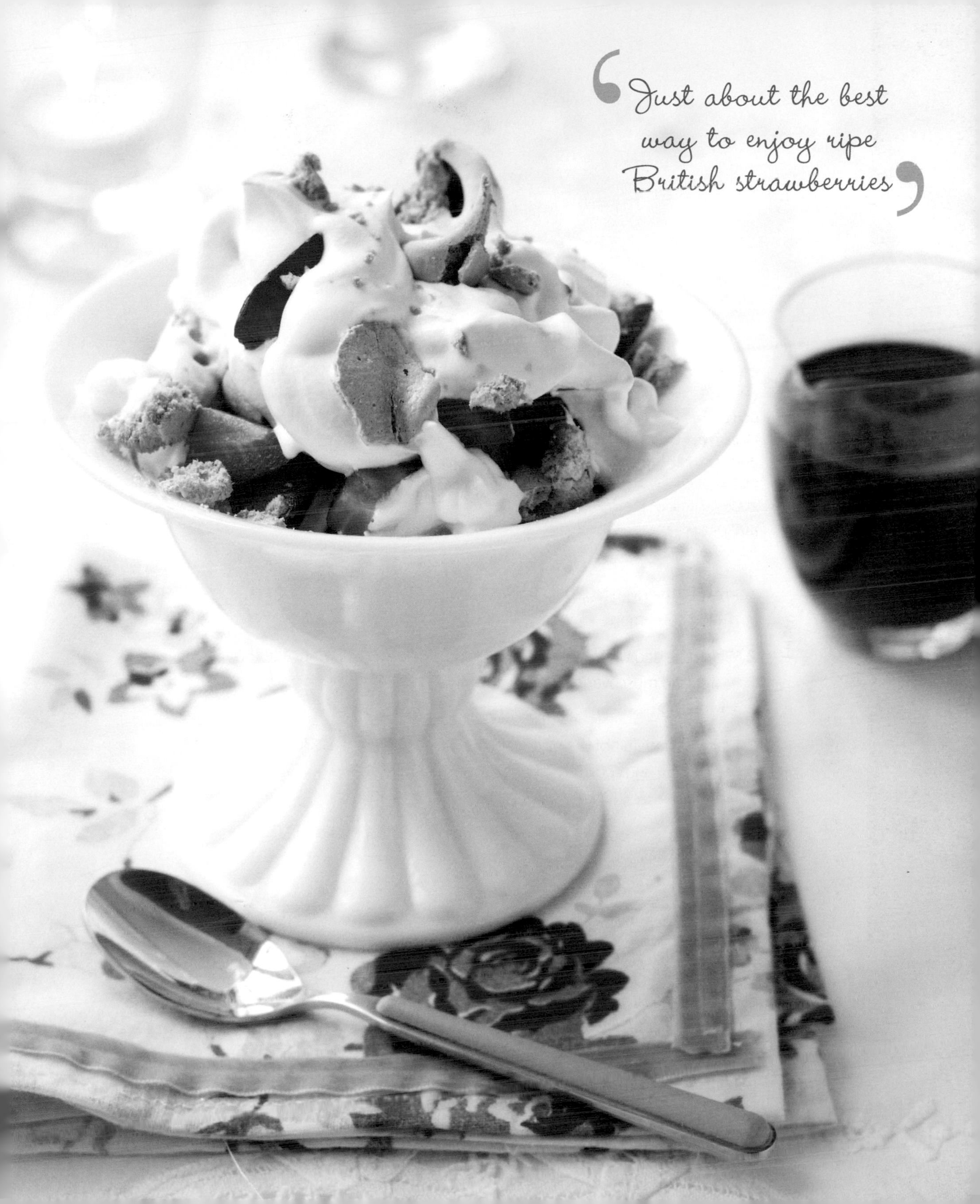
‘Just about the best way to enjoy ripe British strawberries’

Peach & amaretti fool

Serves 4
Prep time: 15 minutes, plus setting time
Cook time: 10 minutes

Baked peaches and the almond flavour of amaretti have a great affinity, and work together perfectly in this fruit fool

4 ripe peaches, stoned and roughly chopped
2 tablespoons runny honey
seeds of 1 vanilla pod

1 x 500g tub Sainsbury's be good to yourself natural Normandy fromage frais
1 tablespoon icing sugar
6 amaretti biscuits

1 Preheat the oven to 180°C, fan 160°C, gas 4.

2 Place the peaches in a roasting tin. Mix the honey with the vanilla pod seeds and drizzle over the peaches. Cook for 10 minutes in the oven, until they're just becoming juicy and golden.

3 Place the fromage frais in a large bowl and sift in the icing sugar, then whisk together. Tip in the peaches and any remaining juices then stir.

4 Divide the fool between 4 glasses and place in the fridge to chill, for up to an hour. Just before serving, crumble the amaretti biscuits over the top of each dessert. Serve immediately, before the biscuits have a chance to go soggy.

Per serving: 120 cals, 0.7g fat, nil sat fat, 25.3g total sugars, 0.2g salt

Crushed amaretti work beautifully with peaches and vanilla in this fool

Serves 12
Prep time: 30 minutes, plus chilling time
Cook time: 40 minutes

V

Chocolate mousse cake

Gorgeously gooey and utterly irresistible, this mousse cake is a chocolate lover's dream

FOR THE SHORTBREAD BASE
240g plain flour
90g caster sugar
170g unsalted butter, cut into small pieces, plus a little extra, for greasing

FOR THE MOUSSE TOPPING
300g dark chocolate
150g unsalted butter
6 eggs, separated
55g caster sugar
cocoa powder, for dusting

1 Preheat the oven to 180°C, fan 160°C, gas 4. Grease a 20cm round springform tin and line with baking parchment.

2 To make the base, place the flour, sugar and butter in a food processor and whizz until it resembles breadcrumbs. Pat together to form a ball, then press the dough evenly into the bottom of the tin. Prick all over with a fork, then bake for about 18-20 minutes, until just dry to the touch. Allow to cool completely, which should take about 30 minutes.

3 To make the mousse topping, place the chocolate and butter in a bowl and melt over a pan of simmering water.

4 Tip the egg whites into a large bowl and whisk until stiff peaks form. In another bowl, whisk the egg yolks with the sugar until pale. Add the chocolate mixture to the egg yolks, then fold in the egg whites.

5 Pour into the cake tin and bake for 15-20 minutes. Allow to cool, then dust with cocoa powder before serving.

Per serving: 504 cals, 34.2g fat, 21.5g sat fat, 24.9g total sugars, 0.1g salt

Did you know...?
Sainsbury's was the first major supermarket to source all its whole eggs from cage-free hens, improving the lives of 800,000 birds

'Rich and decadent,
this cake is the ultimate
chocolate indulgence'

Serves 12
Prep time: 25 minutes
Freeze time: at least
4 hours

V

Ginger parfait

Fresh ginger and crushed ginger biscuits deliver a spicy double whammy
in this delicious frozen dessert

3 large eggs, separated	zest of 1 orange
250g caster sugar	20g fresh ginger, grated
350ml double cream	2 x Sainsbury's ginger snaps, crushed

1 Line a 10 x 25cm loaf tin with clingfilm.

2 Place the egg yolks and 125g sugar in a large bowl and whisk with an electric
   hand mixer, until the mixture is pale and creamy.

3 In another bowl, whip the cream until soft peaks form. In a third bowl,
   whisk the egg whites with the remaining 125g sugar until stiff and glossy.

4 Add the orange zest and grated ginger to the egg yolk mixture. Using
   a rubber spatula, fold in the whipped cream. Finally, gently fold the egg
   whites into the mixture until just combined.

5 Pour into the lined tin and place in the freezer for at least 4 hours, or
   overnight if you have time. It will keep in the freezer for up to 2 weeks.

6 To serve, turn the parfait out onto a plate and top with a sprinkling of
   crushed ginger snaps. Slice and serve immediately.

Per serving: 251 cals, 16g fat, 9.3g sat fat, 23.2g total sugars, trace salt

Cook's note:
this recipe contains raw eggs

Ginger makes this luscious dessert seductively spicy

Summer puddings

Serves 4
Prep time: 20 minutes, plus chilling time
Cook time: 10 minutes

For adults, try replacing the orange juice with Gabriel Boudier crème de cassis

1 x 500g pack Sainsbury's frozen summer fruits
75g caster sugar

2 tablespoons fresh orange juice
8 slices fresh white bread, crusts removed

1 Place the fruit, sugar and orange juice in a pan. Heat over a low heat, until the sugar has dissolved. Bring to a simmer, then remove from the heat.

2 Cut out 4 small and 4 larger discs of bread, using the base and top of a 175ml dariole mould as a guide. Moisten the inside of 4 dariole moulds with a little water. Line with clingfilm, leaving enough to fold over the top. Strain the fruit through a sieve, reserving the syrup.

3 Place a small disc of bread in the bottom of each mould. Cut the remaining bread into big pieces and use to line the sides of the moulds, leaving no gaps.

4 Half-fill each mould with fruit and press down. Drizzle over some syrup and top with the remaining fruit and a little more syrup. Reserve any remaining syrup. Top with the larger discs of bread. Tightly fold over the clingfilm and chill in the fridge for 2-3 hours. To serve, turn out the puddings, discard the clingfilm and drizzle over the remaining syrup. Great with clotted cream.

Per serving: 267 cals, 1.4g fat, nil sat fat, 29.3g total sugars, 0.5g salt

Barbecued nectarines
with mascarpone cream

Preheat the barbecue. In a bowl, whisk together 100g mascarpone, 100g be good to yourself Greek style yogurt and the seeds of 1 vanilla pod. Place 4 halved, stoned nectarines on the barbecue, cut sides down, and cook for 10-15 minutes, until lightly charred and just beginning to soften. Serve with the mascarpone cream, drizzled with 30g runny honey and sprinkled with 20g chopped pistachios.

SERVES 4
Prep time: 10 minutes Cook time: 15 minutes

Per serving:
249 cals, 14.1g fat, 8.5g sat fat, 23.3g total sugars, 0.2g salt

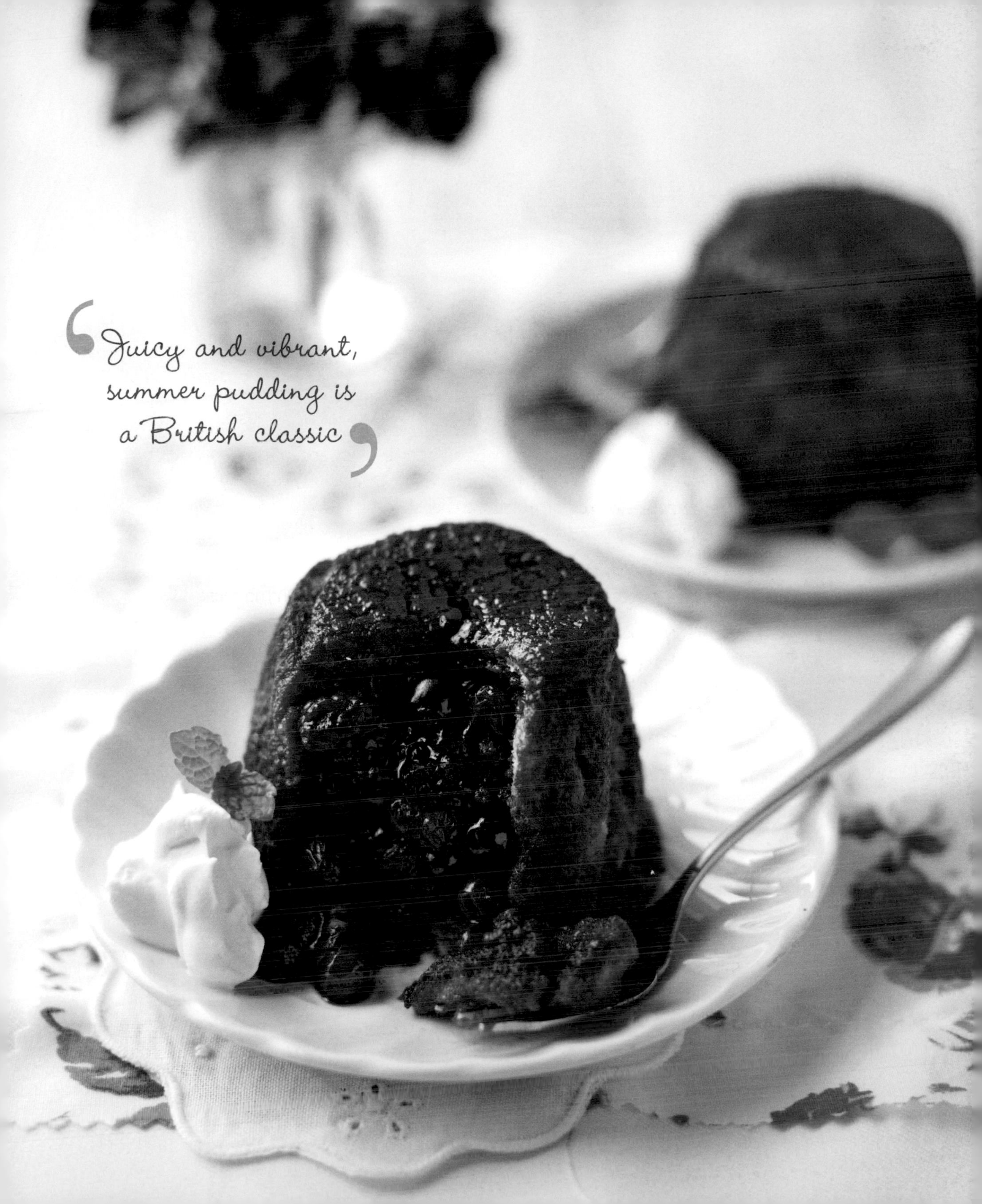

'Juicy and vibrant, summer pudding is a British classic'

Each serves 4
Prep time: 10 minutes,
plus setting time

Cocktail jellies

Fruit cup jelly

1 sachet sugar-free strawberry jelly granules	4 large strawberries, quartered
150ml Pimm's	4 sprigs of mint
350ml lemonade	4 slices of lemon
50g cucumber, finely diced	

1 In a large jug, dissolve the jelly in 100ml boiling water. Leave to cool then pour in the Pimm's and lemonade.

2 Place the cucumber and strawberries in 4 glasses, add a sprig of mint and a lemon slice to each, then pour on the jelly mixture. Place in the fridge to set.

Per serving: 59 cals, 0.1g fat, nil sat fat, 8.6g total sugars, trace salt

Cava, raspberry & orange jelly

1 sachet sugar-free orange jelly granules	50g raspberries, to decorate
500ml Sainsbury's Cava	

1 In a large jug, dissolve the jelly in 100ml boiling water. Leave to cool then pour in enough Cava to make 600ml.

2 Pour into glasses and decorate with raspberries. Place in the fridge to set.

Per serving: 28 cals, trace fat, trace sat fat, 2.3g total sugars, trace salt

Vodka, lime & elderflower jelly

1 sachet sugar-free lemon & lime jelly granules	100ml vodka
50ml elderflower cordial	4 wedges of lime

1 In a large jug, dissolve the jelly in 185ml boiling water. Stir well and add the elderflower and vodka. Add enough cold water to make 600ml and mix well.

2 Place each lime wedge in a glass and pour on the jelly. Place in the fridge to set.

Per serving: 22 cals, trace fat, nil sat fat, 1.6g total sugars, nil salt

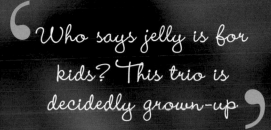

Thai coconut sorbet

Serves 8
Prep time: 15 minutes, plus cooling and freezing time
Cook time: 5 minutes

V

What better way to chill out on a summer's day than with a cool, refreshing scoop of this exotic sorbet...

zest and juice of 3 limes
2 pieces lemon grass, chopped
200g caster sugar
2 red chillies, deseeded and finely chopped

1 ball stem ginger in syrup, drained and finely chopped
1 x 400ml tin coconut milk

1 Place the lime zest, lemon grass, sugar and half the chilli in a pan with 200ml cold water. Stir over a low heat until the sugar has dissolved. Bring to a simmer, then remove from the heat and allow to cool.

2 Once cooled, strain through a sieve and discard the zest, lemon grass and chilli. Add the lime juice, remaining chilli, ginger and coconut milk and stir well. Place the mixture in an ice-cream maker and churn for 1 hour, until frozen. Alternatively, transfer to a freezer-proof container and freeze for 3-4 hours until the mixture has thickened to a sorbet consistency, stirring well every hour. Remove from the freezer 10 minutes before serving.

Per serving: 204 cals, 9g fat, 7.2g sat fat, 28.8g total sugars, trace salt

Serves 6
Prep time: 15 minutes,
plus chilling time

Strawberry marble mousse

Fragrant and juicy British strawberries make the most beautiful desserts, such as this dreamy mousse

400g whole strawberries, hulled and quartered, plus 20 slices to garnish
100g white marshmallows
50g white chocolate

1 x 300ml pot Sainsbury's double cream
1 tablespoon vanilla extract
30g milk chocolate, curled using a peeler

1 Place the strawberries in a microwaveable bowl. Microwave for 3 minutes on high, then roughly mash with a fork and set aside to cool completely.

2 Place the marshmallows and white chocolate in a saucepan with 1 tablespoon water and melt over a low heat. Leave to cool for 1 minute.

3 In a bowl, whisk the double cream with the vanilla extract until soft peaks form. Fold the marshmallow mixture into the cream, then add the cooled strawberries, stirring gently to create a swirl effect.

4 Spoon into glass dishes or coffee cups and top with the strawberry slices and chocolate curls. Chill in the refrigerator for at least 2 hours before serving.

Per serving: 379 cals, 29.3g fat, 16.9g sat fat, 23.3g total sugars, trace salt

Did you know...?
In 2009, Sainsbury's replaced the plastic lids on strawberries with sealed film, saving 333 tonnes of plastic per year

Strawberries and cream are a match made in heaven

Fig & berry no-bake cheesecakes

These delightful little cheesecakes require no baking, and are ideal for anyone following a gluten-free diet

125g hazelnuts, shelled
100g dried, ready-to-eat figs
200g Sainsbury's be good to yourself
Greek style natural yogurt

100g light cream cheese
3 tablespoons caster sugar
4 large strawberries, hulled and sliced
25g blueberries

1 Place the hazelnuts in a food processor and whizz until fine. Add the figs, then whizz until pulped together.

2 Line 4 small tart tins or ramekins with clingfilm, then divide the fig and nut mixture between them, pressing it into the base and up the sides. Place in the freezer for 30–45 minutes.

3 In a bowl, mix together the yogurt and cream cheese until smooth and creamy. Stir in the sugar, then chill in the fridge for 30 minutes.

4 Fill the chilled bases with the cream cheese mixture. Top each cheesecake with strawberry slices and a few blueberries to decorate.

Per serving: 407 cals, 23.1g fat, 3.3g sat fat, 35g total sugars, 0.3g salt

Did you know...?
Sainsbury's freefrom range offers a huge choice of wheat-, gluten- and/or dairy-free foods – all made with only the best ingredients and all surprisingly tasty

"These tasty cheesecakes have bases made from figs and hazelnuts"

Serves 4
Prep time: 30 minutes
Cook time: 1 hour,
20 minutes

Fruit & nut knickerbocker glory

With layers of ice cream, jelly, fresh fruit, meringue and chocolate sauce, a new surprise lies in store with every mouthful

1 medium egg white
55g caster sugar
250g Sainsbury's frozen summer fruit mix, defrosted
1 tablespoon Cointreau (optional)
½ x 300ml pot Sainsbury's whipping cream
1 tablespoon icing sugar
360g vanilla ice cream

1 peach or nectarine, thinly sliced
20g pistachios, chopped

FOR THE CHOCOLATE SAUCE
60g dark chocolate
15g unsalted butter
1 tablespoon golden syrup
1 tablespoon semi-skimmed milk

1 Preheat the oven to 120°C, fan 100°C, gas ½. Line a baking tray with baking parchment.

2 Whisk the egg white in a bowl until soft peaks form, then whisk in the sugar until it's smooth, shiny and holding its shape. Place 4 spoonfuls on the baking tray. Cook in the oven for 1 hour – 1 hour, 15 minutes, until crisp, then remove. Allow to cool, then roughly crush into pieces.

3 Meanwhile, place the defrosted fruit in a bowl. Add the Cointreau and allow to soak for 10-15 minutes. In another bowl, whisk the whipping cream with the icing sugar until peaks form.

4 To make the sauce, place the chocolate, butter, golden syrup and milk in a small pan and melt over a low heat for 5 minutes, stirring until combined.

5 Layer scoops of the whisked cream, summer fruits, crushed meringue, ice cream and slices of peach or nectarine into sundae glasses. Pour over the chocolate sauce and sprinkle with the chopped pistachios.

Per serving: 549 cals, 32.4g fat, 20.1g sat fat, 51g total sugars, 0.3g salt

Time-saving tip
Use ready-made meringues instead of making them

' The ultimate ice cream sundae for every child at heart '

Find the right recipe at a glance

Ⓥ Vegetarian

Asparagus & mozzarella salad	32
Buttered-up corn on the cob	138
Cheese & thyme stuffed mushrooms	60
Cheesy nachos	20
Creamy pea & feta pasta salad	156
Easy sweetcorn relish	138
Fruity & nutty couscous salad	40
Gazpacho	10
Goats' cheese frittata	68
Greek salad	28
Grilled halloumi with sweetcorn relish	134
Guacamole	18
Homemade tomato ketchup	140
Lentil & oat veggie burger	136
Minty broad bean pâté	18
New potato, soya bean & mint salad	156
Noodle salad with stir-fried vegetables	160
Pasta alla Norma	74
Pea & potato gnocchi with fried sage	76
Roasted thyme tomatoes	22
Spiced pitta crisps & houmous	20
Spicy three-bean salad with halloumi	36
Summer vegetable soup with croutons	8
Tomato, red onion & mint salad	44
Two-pea pasta	70
Vegetarian Scotch egg	150
Vietnamese chilli noodles	80
Zesty spring vegetables	58

45 On the table in 45 minutes or less

Artichoke & broad bean salad	38
Asparagus & mozzarella salad	32
Avocado, salami & tomato bruschetta	14
Bacon, asparagus & poached egg salad	46
Barbecued nectarines with mascarpone	178
Barbecued steak with aioli	128
Buttered-up corn on the cob	138
Cheesy nachos	20
Cheese & thyme stuffed mushrooms	60
Coconut fish curry	96
Courgette, pea & parmesan tart	144
Creamy pea & feta pasta salad	156
Crispy fried chicken	148
Easy sweetcorn relish	138
Fruity & nutty couscous salad	40
Fruity bars	162
Gazpacho	10
Goats' cheese frittata	68
Greek salad	28
Griddled sea bass with minty salad	108
Grilled halloumi with sweetcorn relish	134
Grilled sweetcorn, spinach & pancetta salad	30

Gruyère & ham quesadillas	16
Guacamole	18
Herb-crusted roast salmon with mash	88
Herby fish fingers	102
Herby sausage rolls	152
Ice cream snowballs	166
King prawn bake & linguine	110
Lamb & bulgar wheat salad	50
Lamb patties & mint yogurt sauce	122
Minty broad bean pâté	18
Moroccan chicken parcels	124
New potato, soya bean & mint salad	156
Noodle salad with stir-fried vegetables	160
Noodles with roast chicken	56
Oriental stir-fried prawns	92
Paella	62
Pan-fried cod with lemon & olives	84
Pan-fried lime & chilli scallops	98
Pasta alla Norma	74
Peach & amaretti fool	172
Posh hot dogs	126
Prawn, mango & noodle salad	42
Roast monkfish with cherry tomatoes	100
Roast tomato & pesto tagliatelle	62
Rocket & chilli squid salad	48
Salmon & cucumber salad	28
Sea bream with pineapple salsa	114
Seared tuna with salsa verde	104
Sesame chicken & pepper stir-fry	66
Smoked salmon & asparagus niçoise	34
Spiced pitta crisps & houmous	20
Spicy three-bean salad with halloumi	36
Stacked BLT salad	44
Summer vegetable soup with croutons	8
Tomato, red onion & mint salad	44
Tuna with linguine & olives	70
Two-pea pasta	70
Vegetarian Scotch egg	150
Vietnamese chilli noodles	80
Zesty haddock parcels	90
Zesty spring vegetables	58

1-5 1 of 5 a day

Artichoke & broad bean salad	38
Asparagus & mozzarella salad	32
Avocado, salami & tomato bruschetta	14
Barbecued nectarines with mascarpone	178
Broad bean & pea risotto	54
Buttered-up corn on the cob	138
Cheese & thyme stuffed mushrooms	60
Chilli, soy & ginger beef kebabs	130
Classic burger	118
Eton mess	170
Fig & berry no-bake cheesecakes	186

Fish & chips with mushy peas	94
Fruit & nut knickerbocker glory	188
Fruity & nutty couscous salad	40
Greek salad	28
Grilled sweetcorn, spinach & pancetta salad	30
Guacamole	18
Herb-crusted roast salmon with mash	88
Herby turkey burgers	132
Lentil & oat veggie burger	136
Mexican-style meatball wraps	64
Minty broad bean pâté	18
Moroccan chicken parcels	124
Oriental honey roast chicken salad	26
Oriental stir-fried prawns	92
Pan-fried cod with lemon & olives	84
Peach & amaretti fool	172
Roasted thyme tomatoes	22
Rustic fish bake	86
Salmon & cucumber salad	28
Sea bream with pineapple salsa	114
Smoked salmon & asparagus niçoise	34
Soy & citrus salmon salad	106
Stacked BLT salad	44
Summer puddings	178
Summer vegetable soup with croutons	8
Sunshine strawberries	168
Tomato, red onion & mint salad	44
Tuna with linguine & olives	70
Two-pea pasta	70
Vegetarian Scotch egg	150
Zesty haddock parcels	90
Zesty spring vegetables	58

2-5 2 of 5 a day

Butternut squash, bacon & rice salad	158
Coconut fish curry	96
Griddled sea bass with minty salad	108
Lamb & bulgar wheat salad	50
Prosciutto, basil & mozzarella pizzas	78
Roast leg of lamb with turnips & shallots	58
Sesame chicken & pepper stir-fry	66
Spicy three-bean salad with halloumi	36
Sweetcorn chowder with prawns	12
Vietnamese chilli noodles	80

3-5 3 of 5 a day

Gazpacho	10
Noodle salad with stir-fried vegetables	160
Prawn, mango & noodle salad	42
Roast monkfish with cherry tomatoes	100
Smoky beef tacos	72

4-5 4 of 5 a day

Pasta alla Norma	74

Index

Artichoke & broad bean salad 38

Asparagus
Asparagus & mozzarella salad 32
Bacon, asparagus & poached egg salad 46
Smoked salmon & asparagus niçoise 34
Zesty spring vegetables 58

Avocado
Avocado, salami & tomato bruschetta 14
Gruyère & ham quesadillas 16
Guacamole 18
Stacked BLT salad 44

Bacon
Bacon, asparagus & poached egg salad 46
Butternut squash, bacon & rice salad 158
Stacked BLT salad 44
Barbecued nectarines with mascarpone 178
Barbecued steak with aioli 128

Beef
Barbecued steak with aioli 128
Chilli, soy & ginger beef kebabs 130
Classic burger 118
Mexican-style meatball wraps 64
Smoky beef tacos 72

Broad beans
Artichoke & broad bean salad 38
Broad bean & pea risotto 54
Minty broad bean pâté 18
Zesty spring vegetables 58

Burgers
Classic burger 118
Herby turkey burgers 132
Lentil & oat veggie burger 136
Buttered-up corn on the cob 138
Butternut squash, bacon & rice salad 158
Cava, raspberry & orange jelly 180

Cheese
Asparagus & mozzarella salad 32
Cheese & thyme stuffed mushrooms 60
Cheesy nachos 20
Chorizo, manchego & pepper stratas 152
Courgette & cheese frittata 154
Courgette, pea & parmesan tart 144
Creamy pea & feta pasta salad 156
Fig & berry no-bake cheesecakes 186
Goats' cheese frittata 68

Greek salad 28
Grilled halloumi with sweetcorn relish 134
Gruyère & ham quesadillas 16
Minty broad bean pâté 18
Prosciutto, basil & mozzarella pizzas 78
Spicy three-bean salad with halloumi 36

Chicken
Crispy fried chicken 148
Grilled Caesar chicken skewers 120
Moroccan chicken parcels 124
Noodles with roast chicken 56
Oriental honey roast chicken salad 26
Sesame chicken & pepper stir-fry 66
Sweet soy chicken drumsticks 148

Chilli
Chilli, soy & ginger beef kebabs 130
Noodles with roast chicken 56
Pan-fried lime & chilli scallops 98
Rocket & chilli squid salad 48
Vietnamese chilli noodles 80

Chocolate
Chocky rocky road 162
Chocolate mousse cake 174
Chorizo, manchego & pepper stratas 152
Classic burger 118
Cocktail jellies 180
Coconut fish curry 96

Courgette
Courgette & cheese frittata 154
Courgette, pea & parmesan tart 144
Zesty spring vegetables 58

Couscous
Asparagus & mozzarella salad 32
Fruity & nutty couscous salad 40
Moroccan chicken parcels 124
Creamy pea & feta pasta salad 156
Crispy fried chicken 148

Desserts
Barbecued nectarines 178
Cava, raspberry & orange jelly 180
Chocolate mousse cake 174
Cocktail jellies 180
Eton mess 170
Fig & berry no-bake cheesecakes 186
Fruit cup jelly 180

Ginger parfait 176
Ice cream snowballs 166
Fruit & nut knickerbocker glory 188
Peach & amaretti fool 172
Strawberry marble mousse 184
Summer berry jelly 168
Summer puddings 178
Sunshine strawberries 168
Super-simple vanilla ice cream 166
Thai coconut sorbet 182
Vodka, lime & elderflower jelly 180
Easy sweetcorn relish 138

Eggs
Bacon, asparagus & poached egg salad 46
Courgette & cheese frittata 154
Goats' cheese frittata 68
Vegetarian Scotch egg 150
Eton mess 170
Fig & berry no-bake cheesecakes 186

Fish
Coconut fish curry 96
Fish & chips with mushy peas 94
Griddled sea bass with minty salad 108
Herb-crusted roast salmon with mash 88
Herby fish fingers 102
Pan-fried cod with lemon & olives 84
Roast monkfish with cherry tomatoes 100
Rustic fish bake 86
Salmon & cucumber salad 28
Salmon & red onion fishcakes 112
Sea bream with pineapple salsa 114
Seared tuna with salsa verde 104
Smoked mackerel pâté 22
Smoked salmon & asparagus niçoise 34
Soy & citrus salmon salad 106
Tuna with linguine & olives 70
Zesty haddock parcels 90
Fruit & nut knickerbocker glory 188
Fruit cup jelly 180
Fruity & nutty couscous salad 40
Fruity bars 162
Gazpacho 10
Ginger parfait 176
Goats' cheese frittata 68
Greek salad 28

Griddled sea bass with minty salad	108	King prawn bake & linguine	110	Paella	62
Grilled Caesar chicken skewers	120	Pasta alla Norma	74	Roast leg of lamb with turnips & shallots	58
Grilled halloumi with sweetcorn relish	134	Pea & potato gnocchi with fried sage	76	Roast monkfish with cherry tomatoes	100
Grilled sweetcorn, spinach		Roast tomato & pesto tagliatelle	62	Roast tomato & pesto tagliatelle	62
& pancetta salad	30	Tuna with linguine & olives	70	Roasted thyme tomatoes	22
Gruyère & ham quesadillas	16	Two-pea pasta	70	Rocket & chilli squid salad	48
Guacamole	18	Peach & amaretti fool	172	Rustic fish bake	86
Herb-crusted roast salmon with mash	88	**Peas**		**Salads**	
Herby fish fingers	102	Broad bean & pea risotto	54	Artichoke & broad bean salad	38
Herby sausage rolls	152	Courgette, pea & parmesan tart	144	Asparagus & mozzarella salad	32
Herby turkey burgers	132	Creamy pea & feta pasta salad	156	Bacon, asparagus & poached egg salad	46
Homemade barbecue sauce	140	Mushy peas	94	Butternut squash, bacon & rice salad	158
Homemade houmous	126	Pea & potato gnocchi with fried sage	76	Creamy pea & feta pasta salad	156
Homemade tomato ketchup	140	Two-pea pasta	70	Fruity & nutty couscous salad	40
Ice cream		Zesty spring vegetables	58	Greek salad	28
Ice cream snowballs	166	Pineapple salsa	114	Grilled sweetcorn, spinach	
Super-simple vanilla ice cream	166	**Pizza**		& pancetta salad	30
Jelly		Prosciutto, basil & mozzarella pizzas	78	Lamb & bulgar wheat salad	50
Cava, raspberry & orange jelly	180	Posh hot dogs	126	New potato, soya bean & mint salad	156
Fruit cup jelly	180	**Pork**		Noodle salad with stir-fried vegetables	160
Summer berry jelly	168	Herby sausage rolls	152	Oriental honey roast chicken salad	26
Vodka, lime & elderflower jelly	180	Little pork & apricot parcels	146	Prawn, mango & noodle salad	42
King prawn bake & linguine	110	Pork, sage & leek kebabs	130	Rocket & chilli squid salad	48
Lamb		Posh hot dogs	126	Salmon & cucumber salad	28
Lamb & bulgar wheat salad	50	**Potatoes**		Smoked mackerel pâté	22
Lamb patties & mint yogurt sauce	122	Courgette & cheese frittata	154	Smoked salmon & asparagus niçoise	34
Roast leg of lamb with turnips & shallots	58	Fish & chips with mushy peas	94	Soy & citrus salmon salad	106
Lentil & oat veggie burger	136	New potato, soya bean & mint salad	156	Spicy three-bean salad with halloumi	36
Little pork & apricot parcels	146	Pea & potato gnocchi with fried sage	76	Stacked BLT salad	44
Mexican-style meatball wraps	64	**Prawns**		Tomato, red onion & mint salad	44
Minty broad bean pâté	18	King prawn bake & linguine	110	**Salmon**	
Moroccan chicken parcels	124	Oriental stir-fried prawns	92	Herb-crusted roast salmon with mash	88
New potato, soya bean & mint salad	156	Prawn, mango & noodle salad	42	Salmon & cucumber salad	28
Noodles		Sweetcorn chowder with prawns	12	Salmon & red onion fishcakes	112
Noodle salad with stir-fried vegetables	160	Prosciutto, basil & mozzarella pizzas	78	Smoked salmon & asparagus niçoise	34
Noodles with roast chicken	56	**Relishes**		Soy & citrus salmon salad	106
Prawn, mango & noodle salad	42	Homemade barbecue sauce	140	Salsa verde	104
Vietnamese chilli noodles	80	Homemade tomato ketchup	140	Sea bream with pineapple salsa	114
Oriental honey roast chicken salad	26	Pineapple salsa	114	**Seafood**	
Oriental stir-fried prawns	92	Salsa verde	104	Griddled sea bass with minty salad	108
Paella	62	Spicy radish, apple & sweetcorn relish	134	King prawn bake & linguine	110
Pan-fried cod with lemon & olives	84	Tartare sauce	94	Oriental stir-fried prawns	92
Pan-fried lime & chilli scallops	98	**Rice**		Paella	62
Pasta		Broad bean & pea risotto	54	Pan-fried lime & chilli scallops	98
Creamy pea & feta pasta salad	156	Butternut squash, bacon & rice salad	158	Prawn, mango & noodle salad	42

Sweetcorn chowder with prawns	12
Seared tuna with salsa verde	104
Sesame chicken & pepper stir-fry	66
Smoked mackerel pâté	22
Smoked salmon & asparagus niçoise	34
Smoky beef tacos	72
Soups	
Gazpacho	10
Summer vegetable soup with croutons	8
Sweetcorn chowder with prawns	12
Soy & citrus salmon salad	106
Spiced pitta crisps & houmous	20
Spicy radish, apple & sweetcorn relish	134
Spicy three-bean salad with halloumi	36
Stacked BLT salad	44
Strawberries	
Eton mess	170
Fig & berry no-bake cheesecakes	186
Strawberry marble mousse	184
Sunshine strawberries	168
Summer berry jelly	168
Summer puddings	178
Summer vegetable soup with croutons	8
Sunshine strawberries	168
Super-simple vanilla ice cream	166
Sweet soy chicken drumsticks	148
Sweetcorn chowder with prawns	12
Tartare sauce	94
Thai coconut sorbet	182
Tomatoes	
Avocado, salami & tomato bruschetta	14
Homemade tomato ketchup	140
Roast tomato & pesto tagliatelle	62
Roasted thyme tomatoes	22
Stacked BLT salad	44
Tomato, red onion & mint salad	44
Tuna	
Seared tuna with salsa verde	104
Tuna with linguine & olives	70
Two-pea pasta	70
Vegetarian Scotch egg	150
Vietnamese chilli noodles	80
Vodka, lime & elderflower jelly	180
Zesty haddock parcels	90
Zesty spring vegetables	58

Conversion table

Weights		Volume		Measurements		Oven temperatures		fan	gas
15g	½ oz	25ml	1fl oz	2mm	1/16 in	110°C	90°C		
25g	1oz	50ml	2fl oz	3mm	1/8 in	120°C	100°C	½	
40g	1½ oz	75ml	3fl oz	4mm	1/6 in	140°C	120°C	1	
50g	2oz	100ml	4fl oz	5mm	¼ in	150°C	130°C	2	
60g	2½ oz	150ml	5fl oz (¼ pint)	1cm	½ in	160°C	140°C	3	
75g	3oz	175ml	6fl oz	2cm	¾ in	180°C	160°C	4	
100g	3½ oz	200ml	7fl oz	2.5cm	1in	190°C	170°C	5	
125g	4oz	225ml	8fl oz	3cm	1¼ in	200°C	180°C	6	
150g	5oz	250ml	9fl oz	4cm	1½ in	220°C	200°C	7	
175g	6oz	300ml	10fl oz (½ pint)	4.5cm	1¾ in	230°C	210°C	8	
200g	7oz	350ml	13fl oz	5cm	2in	240°C	220°C	9	
225g	8oz	400ml	14fl oz	6cm	2½ in				
250g	9oz	450ml	16fl oz (¾ pint)	7.5cm	3in				
275g	10oz	600ml	20fl oz (1 pint)	9cm	3½ in				
300g	11oz	750ml	25fl oz (1¼ pints)	10cm	4in				
350g	12oz	900ml	30fl oz (1½ pints)	13cm	5in				
375g	13oz	1 litre	34fl oz (1¾ pints)	13.5cm	5¼ in				
400g	14oz	1.2 litres	40fl oz (2 pints)	15cm	6in				
425g	15oz	1.5 litres	52fl oz (2½ pints)	16cm	6½ in				
450g	1lb	1.8 litres	60fl oz (3 pints)	18cm	7in				
500g	1lb 2oz			19cm	7½ in				
650g	1lb 7oz			20cm	8in				
675g	1½ lb			23cm	9in				
700g	1lb 9oz			24cm	9½ in				
750g	1lb 11oz			25.5cm	10in				
900g	2lb			28cm	11in				
1kg	2lb 4oz			30cm	12in				
1.5kg	3lb 6oz			32.5cm	13in				
				35cm	14in				

Seven.

© Produced by Seven Publishing on behalf of Sainsbury's Supermarkets Ltd, 33 Holborn, London EC1N 2HT.
Published March 2011. All rights reserved. No part of this publication may be reproduced, stored in a retrieval system or transmitted in any form by any means, electronic, mechanical, photocopying, recording or otherwise, without the prior written permission of Seven Publishing. Printed and bound by Butler Tanner & Dennis Ltd, Frome and London. ISBN-13: 978-0956630322

Credits

Food
Senior food editor Georgina Fuggle
Food assistant Mima Sinclair
Food assistant Hannah Yeadon

Design
Senior art director David Jenkins
Designer Nina Brennan
Stylist Morag Farquhar

Editorial
Editor Jo Clifton

Account management
Senior account director Lynne de Lacy
Account executive Amy Fixter
Publishing director Dorcas Jamieson
Head of content Helen Renshaw

Photography
Gareth Morgans, Dan Jones,
Kate Whitaker, Craig Robertson

For Sainsbury's
Book team Phil Carroll, Louise Chipps,
Richard Crampton
Nutrition Annie Denny, Becky Williams
Own-brand team Susan Judge,
Susi Richards
Marketing team Rebecca Singleton,
Sheetal Meakin, Katarina Williams

Print & production
Production manager Mike Lamb
Colour origination F1 Colour Ltd
Printers Butler Tanner & Dennis Ltd,
Frome and London

Special thanks to...
Valerie Barrett, Sal Henley, Cara Hobday,
Denise Smart, Elaine Gowran, Nicky
Gyopari, Sam Stowell, Phillip Webb, Clare
Miller, Geoff Fenney, Terry Benson, Lis
Parsons, Patricia Baker, Nina Christopher,
Caroline Tennent, Lucy Rainer

Seven.

MIX
Paper from
responsible sources
FSC® C023561
www.fsc.org

GREAT BRITISH BOOKS
PUBLISHED & PRINTED IN THE UK